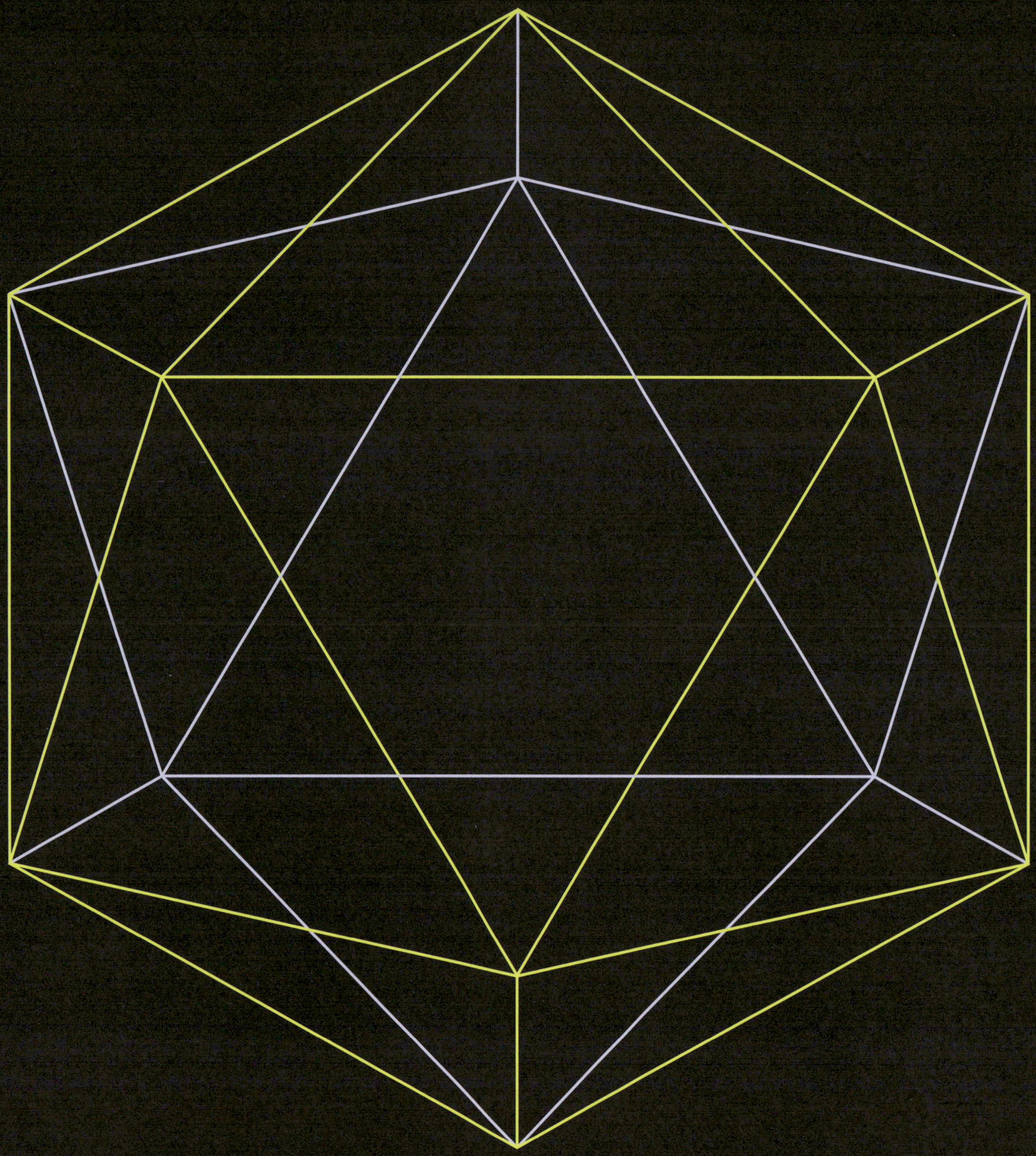

RUSH&2112

RUSH

RUSH & 2112

FIFTY YEARS

Daniel Bukszpan

PLYMOUTH MICH. WELCOME'S
RUSH
TOURING NORTH AMERICA 1977

CONTENTS

On May 22, 1977, fans at the McMorran Arena in Port Huron, Michigan, wait for Rush to do that thing they do so well.

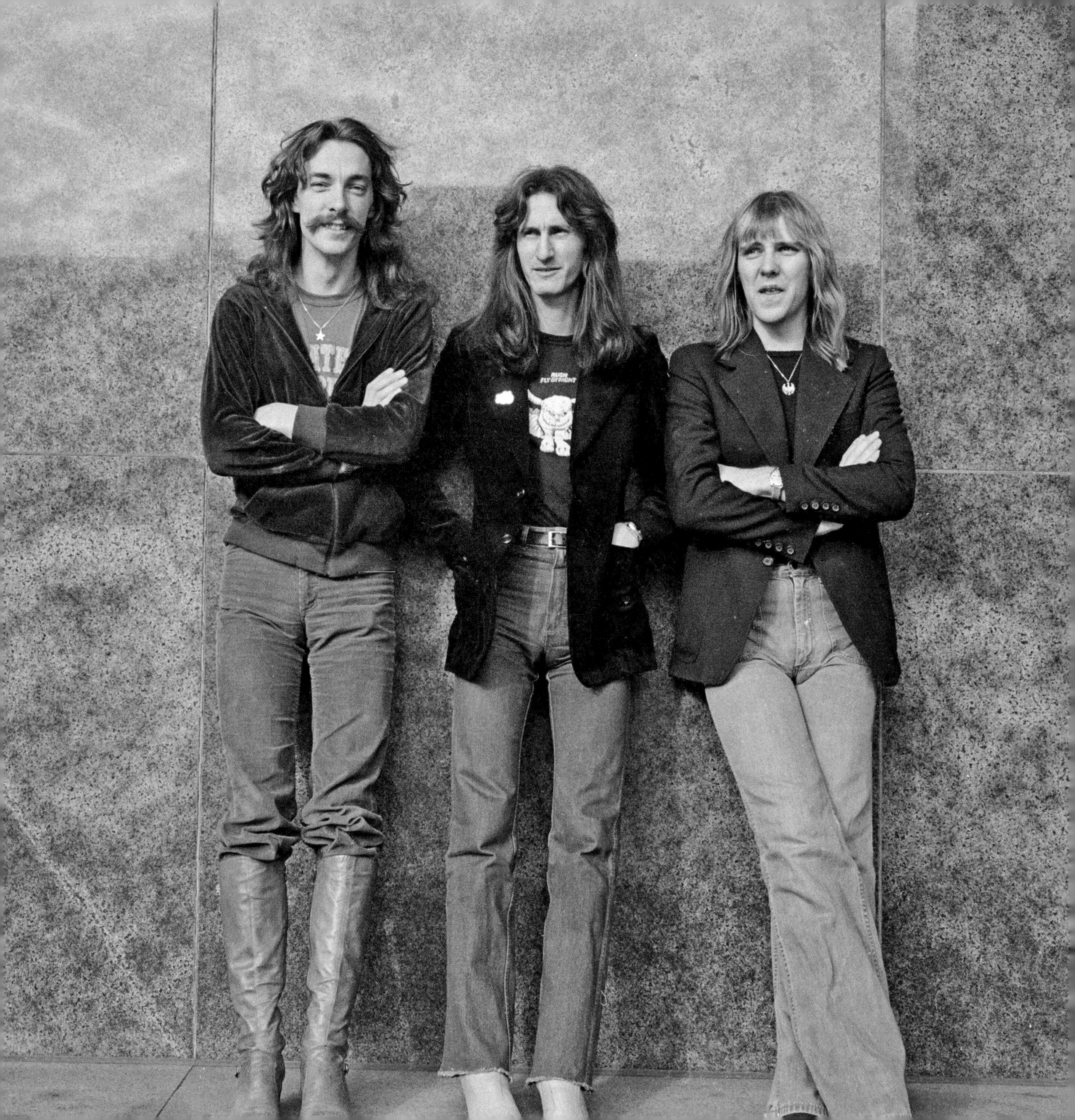

INTRODUCTION

Neil Peart, Geddy Lee, and Alex Lifeson (L-R) strike a pose on December 17, 1977, in Cleveland, Ohio, the city that gave them their breakthrough in the States.

***2112* WAS RUSH'S FOURTH STUDIO ALBUM.** Released in 1976, it was their commercial breakthrough and established them as one of the most popular bands in the world, a status they still enjoy today. Despite making their final studio album in 2012, we're not done with Rush. We may never be.

We're not done with them because the music they created was so rich and complex that it always pays off, no matter how many times you listen to it. You can always go deeper on the next listen, and that's because there's so much depth to their music, the lyrics, and the themes they explored.

The group's 1974 self-titled debut album was a straightforward and uninhibited rocker that gave no indication of the band they would become. The drummer on that record, John Rutsey, took his leave from the band, making it necessary for bassist Geddy Lee and guitarist Alex Lifeson to replace him. Their ultimate choice after a few auditions was Neil Peart. Not only was he the greatest drummer who ever lived, but he also wrote lyrics, which were like nothing before or since.

Everyone who knew the drummer described him as a big reader, and indeed, he was happy to be tucked away in some well-lit corner of the room, absorbing meaty tomes that casual readers would abandon after seeing nothing more than the title on the spine. He took it all in ravenously; it informed his lyrics, and to this day, no one has ever come close to copying what he did.

With Peart in the band, Rush first created *Fly by Night* and *Caress of Steel*, two inspired 1975 albums made by a band still searching for their identity. They found it on their fourth LP. It's where they found their voice and then refined it. It's where they transcended their influences and became something distinct. *2112* is where Rush discovered their identity, and they ran with it.

The title track is a futuristic, dystopian epic taking up all of side one. It tells the story of an individual living in a police state, and its lyrics are nightmare fuel reminiscent of the most anxiety-provoking episode of *Black Mirror*. It depicts a world no one would ever want to live in and takes a full album side to do it.

Their label, Mercury Records, initially had hoped for a single from this record. They didn't get one, and history has proven that twenty-minute sagas about space dystopias have never made the top 40—nor will they ever. Nonetheless, a strange thing happened. This record, which was not commercial by any standard, became the group's hottest seller yet. It defied every conceivable bit of conventional wisdom.

Rush had toured heavily since Peart joined the band, so much of the breakthrough they experienced with *2112* resulted from their road regimen. Still, something about this record—

something beyond the tunes—made it connect with listeners. The music was complex but direct, and the lyrics about a lone individual facing off against conformity were something almost anyone could relate to.

The three members of Rush were uncompromising in their pursuit of stylistic change, so you can't really say there's a "Rush sound." Sure, there's Geddy Lee's voice, an instrument never replicated by any other singer (although Michigan singer-songwriter Patty PerShayla has come very close on many occasions); but otherwise, there is no "Rush sound." It always changed. Having said that, the band's hallmarks of instrumental virtuosity and literature-inspired lyrics are fully realized for the first time on *2112*; so if you want to argue for the existence of a "Rush sound," this would be the starting point.

2112 can also be said to be one of the highest peaks Rush attained while working with co-producer Terry Brown. The band's management brought him in to help them finish their self-titled debut, and after that, they would make eight more studio albums together, all classics up to and including 1982's *Signals*.

After parting ways with Brown, Rush still made some truly monumental albums with several different people at the mixing desk. The run of albums the band made with Brown, however, is really, really hard to beat. They all have a certain quality that is absent from later albums, and no one can quite put their finger on what that is. It may simply be that the band and the co-producer were young and excited to be making records, and that enthusiasm spilled over into them.

It may also be that all the records they made with Brown were built upon basic tracks performed live as a band, with vocals and other touches overdubbed later. When you record live, you're just going to get a little something extra that you can't get with a click track. It simply will not be there if the band members record their parts separately, no matter how skilled the producer. Every record the band made with Terry Brown was recorded as a band, and that goes a long way.

While *2112* marked a beginning for Rush, it also marked an ending. It was the last time they relied almost entirely on a raw power trio sound on a studio record. Apart from some keyboard contributions from album cover designer Hugh Syme, what we hear on *2112* is the raw bass, drums, and guitar configuration of Rush—something they began to move away from on subsequent records. But even those subsequent records are built on basic tracks cut by three guys who loved playing together as a band, and that energy is present on *2112* from start to finish.

This is not my first rodeo when writing about this band. My book *Rush at 50* was released in 2024, and as I was doing the publicity rounds for it on various podcasts, I realized why the story of Rush—particularly the story of making *2112*—is so compelling.

No one wanted them to make the album, no one encouraged them, and the record company could have pulled the plug on the whole enterprise at any moment. It was an existentially stressful moment for this band, but rather than tear themselves apart over the issue of their relative commerciality, they circled the wagons. They drew closer to each other. They resolved to be true to their vision even if it meant the end of the band, and the story of three people with ironclad belief in their vision—and each other—will always be compelling.

Gene Simmons of KISS made a similar point in an article called, "'I Was Trying to Get Them Laid.'" Rush and KISS played together quite a bit between 1974 and 1976, and during that time, Simmons and his bandmates were front-row witnesses to the trio's transformation from a "Led Zeppelin Junior" hard rock band to something else entirely. He said Peart had been the catalyst for that transformation.

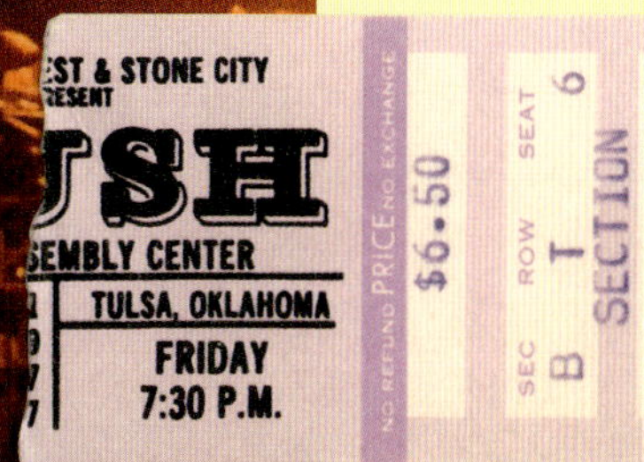

CLOCKWISE, FROM ABOVE Alex Lifeson, bathed in red, helps bring the story of the poor, beleaguered Anonymous narrator to the people.

On April 14, 1977, American prog rockers Starcastle lived many bands' worst nightmare–opening for Rush–at Memorial Coliseum in Fort Wayne, Indiana.

One of the ambitious, full-spread print advertisements Mercury Records ran in newspapers to advertise what Rush feared might be their final album.

Geddy Lee gives the people what they want at the Nelson Center in Springfield, Illinois, on May 15, 1977.

"Neil read lots of books, and started to bring in that sci-fi, Isaac Asimov kind of thing," Simmons said. "Plus, he knew lots of big words, like 'condominium.'"

While the bassist always preferred the band's more straightforward early material, one thing he said never changed about them was their commitment to their artistic vision and to each other. Since radio wanted nothing to do with them, this meant touring relentlessly—and the Canadian power trio understood that.

"Before MTV, cellphones, and iPads, there were only three or four TV stations and a few radio stations," Simmons said. "The only way to get your music out there was to go to the people."

Rush did precisely that. Even in the middle of his own groupie-swathed bacchanalia, Simmons was able to see that Lee, Lifeson, and Peart were deadly serious about doing the hard work it took to get to the next level. The rock-and-roll lifestyle had its share of temptations and pitfalls, and endless horror stories exist of the many talented musicians who lost focus and succumbed to it, sometimes fatally. The KISS bassist said that Rush managed to steer clear of that even in the early days, and he invoked Alexandre Dumas' *The Three Musketeers* to make that point.

"They were 'all for one and one for all,'" he said.

Decades later, *2112* is still considered one of Rush's best efforts and one of the greatest concept albums ever made. The band caught a lot of flak for dedicating it to author Ayn Rand, a significant inspiration to Peart in crafting the title suite's lyrics and overall theme. They even got called proponents of the Third Reich's philosophy for it, a mendacious smear that stuck for decades.

2112 outlasted it. Rush outlasted it, and they outlasted the dude who said it. The guy is still alive at the time of this writing, but it's probably safe to say that many more people have read the lyrics to "2112" than any of his articles. Furthermore, many who read his articles were Rush fans, who came away even more determined to stand by the group. The critics have never understood that their own criticisms have only made Rush fans dig in deeper and made them even prouder to champion the group. After all, when someone attacks something you love, you will defend it.

None of the changes in today's technology, culture, or politics that have come since 1976 have diminished the album's importance or immediacy. The music is still like nothing else ever made, which also goes for the lyrics. Since its release, countless artists have said they were influenced by it, that it changed their lives, that its story made them determined to live out their dreams despite stiff opposition. That's why the listening public is not done with *2112*, and as long as people have dreams that those in authority wish to thwart, *2112* will always be relevant.

SECTOR ONE

"Attention planets of the Solar Federation...Alex Lifeson, Neil Peart, and Geddy Lee have assumed control."

OVERTURE

THE STORY OF HOW RUSH MADE *2112* is in many ways the story of their association with co-producer Terry Brown. He and the band had a fruitful partnership that lasted for almost a decade and spanned nine studio albums, all considered indispensable pillars of the group's catalog today.

Rush craved growth and change on every album. The band always strived to evolve, so each album they made throughout their career was intended to sound different from the previous one. Still, if you had to describe an era of the band as the "classic" era, the period between 1974 and 1982 covers it for many people.

The band's first three albums were all bangers. This is a proven scientific fact that has been subjected to a withering peer review process by fans over five decades, and the jury is in—those are outstanding records. There's no denying that *2112*, however, was their first significant milestone. In 2016, no less an authority than the band's own guitarist Alex Lifeson told *Classic Rock* that *2112* was the album where Rush first sounded like Rush.

"*2112* was the first album where we really felt like we had an identifiable sound," he said.

After the association between the band and Brown ended, Rush went on to work with different producers. Brown went on to work with other artists as well, and both excelled in their respective efforts. Still, there's just something about that Brown-helmed run of albums that the trio worked on—there's a particular mood and atmosphere, and it's only present on those records.

Their later career is full of excellent albums like *Grace under Pressure*, *Presto*, *Vapor Trails*, and their swan song, *Clockwork Angels*, to name just a few. But for those of us of a certain age who came to the band at a certain time, their collaborations with Terry Brown grabbed us like no other music did. It made us lifers, and we returned to those albums again and again. And while all those nine albums are masterpieces, *2112* is right up there with *Moving Pictures* as one of the band's greatest works.

LEFT A likely unofficial but nonetheless cool comic-style rendering of what one assumes are Father Brown's acolytes standing in front of the brain from the cover of 1978's *Hemispheres* album.

1

THE HOLY TRINITY

2

I. GEDDY LEE

Rush bassist and vocalist Geddy Lee was born on July 29, 1953, in Willowdale, a Toronto neighborhood that also served as the birthplace for such luminaries as Corey Haim and Howie Mandel. He was born to Morris and Mary Weinrib, Jewish immigrants from Poland.

In 2019, Lee told New York City radio station Q104.3 that his parents met in a Nazi work camp when they were both barely teenagers. They were eventually sent to the Auschwitz concentration camp before being separated and shipped off to separate facilities, presumably never to see one another again. Somehow, against extremely steep odds, they reunited at a displaced persons camp at Bergen-Belsen at the end of World War II and were eventually liberated.

"My earliest memories were my mother talking about the war and talking about Hitler and about what had happened to her family," Lee said. "I remember my mother constantly reinforcing the idea that we had to keep the family together because these terrible things can happen."

Lee was only 12 when his father passed away at the age of 45, forcing his mother to start working and support the family. This left him and his siblings in the care of their grandmother while Mary was making ends meet.

"BACK IN MY DAY, NOBODY CHOSE TO BE THE BASS PLAYER . . . YOU WERE ALWAYS A GUITARIST, AND SOMEBODY SAID, 'WELL, WE NEED A BASS PLAYER,' SO THEY HAD A VOTE AND YOU BECAME THE BASS PLAYER."

GEDDY LEE
to *Rolling Stone*, 2020

BELOW Geddy Lee in 1977, bordered by big, beautiful, backstage basses.

PREVIOUS The scene of the crime. Rush at London's Hammersmith Odeon in 1979, one year after a notorious interview at that venue suggested Neil Peart hoped you would get sick and die in the street if you didn't sleep on a bed made of money.

By age 14, his interest in listening to music led him to start playing guitar. Ultimately, he switched to bass, which was not entirely his choice—it could even be classified as a demotion in some quarters.

"Back in my day, nobody chose to be the bass player," Geddy Lee told *Rolling Stone* in 2020. "You were always a guitarist, and somebody said, 'Well, we need a bass player,' so they had a vote and you became the bass player."

Despite the semi-voluntary nature of the change of instruments, Lee said he took to it immediately. If he had initially viewed it as a demotion, it didn't last long.

"I adapted to it very quickly and really loved it," he said.

Lee's decision to become a bassist was perfectly timed as it coincided with the psychedelic movement. Musicians such as Cream's Jack Bruce approached the bass in revolutionary new ways, transforming it from a background instrument that only held down root notes. He and others, like the Who's John Entwistle, expanded the definition of what a bass could do, making it an equal contributor to the song alongside the guitar and vocals. Lee said that being in a power trio made that approach a necessity.

"The bass player has a bigger role in that format, especially when the lead guitarist is soloing," he said. "You have to provide enough noise behind him to keep it from sounding empty. So it's a license to be a bit obnoxious, which I always appreciated."

Lee also cited the mighty Chris Squire of Yes as a significant influence. A friend had played him the song "No Opportunity Necessary, No Experience Needed" off the band's 1970 *Time and a Word* album, and if you've ever heard it, then you know the bass performance is a propulsive beast that will not be ignored. It's mixed even louder than the guitar on that record.

Lee knew he wanted to commit to a life in music, but it might not have happened if his father had still been alive. He characterized Morris Weinrib as a tough customer with a strong presence, and maybe anyone who had experienced the horrors of the Holocaust firsthand at a young age would have turned out the same.

Lee said his father might have forbidden him from leaving school to pursue playing music professionally, and he had been such an imposing figure that his bass-obsessed son might have listened. Still, he couldn't deny that his father's passing, while emotionally devastating, also created a power vacuum in his family's home allowing him to commit to music full-time.

Before too long, the basement in his home became a rehearsal space, where he and his like-minded musician friends could jam for hours, doing so loudly and often, much to his grandmother's chagrin. Once Lee began earning a little money from performances, he dropped out of high school to pursue music full-time.

Lee acknowledged that his decision had disappointed his mother, who initially felt it was a *shanda*. At the same time, it was, in some ways, a tribute to his late father; the man had experienced a lot of suffering and persevered through it all, only to have his life end at age 45. It seemed unjust, to say the very least.

"All that work and all that grief, and he got ripped off at an early age," he said of his father. "I think that's why I just want to keep playing. . . . While I have my faculties, I want to enjoy everything there is, see as much as I can, just make the most of life."

He legally changed his name to Geddy Lee, immortalizing his Polish mother's accented pronunciation of "Gary." He also inherited the role of lead singer, the other position in a band besides "bass player" that nobody wants. In 2015, he told *Rolling Stone* that the lead vocalist slot was also something he won by default.

"Nobody wanted to sing, so they always said, 'You do the singing,'" he said. "I liked singing, but I liked playing bass more and I still do."

He said he had been influenced by singers such as Steve Marriott of Humble Pie and John Anderson of Yes, who sang in high vocal ranges. Lee sang in a distinct, high-pitched register that some mistook for Led Zeppelin's Robert Plant early on. Others, meanwhile, absolutely hated it and still complain about it to this day, characterizing it as shrill and screechy.

The critics were determined to be complete jerks about it—a pursuit they engaged in relentlessly—causing them to perseverate on this particular issue. Maybe someone had hit them over the head with a folding chair, and now all they could do was write "brittle and androgynous" over and over again until they hit their word count.

Your mileage may vary, but Dr. R. Douglas Helvering, composer and host of the *Daily Doug* YouTube channel, said these critics had it all wrong. Lee's voice, while certainly not to everyone's taste, is the right tool for the job, in his view.

"Geddy just has one of those unique voices," he said. "It's in the way that his face is structured, the size of his nose, all of it comes into play with the resonance that he specifically has. It's got a bright quality to it, but he's also got a little bit of a hooded quality."

He added that many people over the years have flung disparaging adjectives Lee's way to register displeasure with the way he sounds. The real adjective that should be used to describe it, however, is "*strident*," which Merriam-Webster defines as "characterized by harsh, insistent, and discordant sound" and "commanding attention by a loud or obtrusive quality." He doesn't mean it in a bad way, though.

"Sometimes music needs something, an instrument that makes a strident sound, to make the overall thing work," he said.

Throughout his career with Rush and beyond, Lee would be recognized as the world-class artist that he is. He's influenced countless musi-

Geddy Lee operates a Minimoog on December 2, 1978. Rush had begun expanding on their power trio arrangements and incorporating other textures, to the eventual chagrin of some.

Rickenb

cians, including Metallica's Cliff Burton and Iron Maiden's Steve Harris, who seemed to take his attention-grabbing, intricate, and overdriven style to heart.

He's come a long way since the days of jamming in his grandmother's basement, and *2112* is where listeners can see him lay the groundwork for becoming the fully developed artist who would emerge on subsequent records. In later years, he would sing in a lower pitch and smooth out many of his bass's rough edges; but at the time of *2112*, his approach to both was aggressive and extreme, and took no prisoners.

II. ALEX LIFESON

Rush guitarist Alex Lifeson was born on August 27, 1953. His real name is Aleksandar Živojinović, and he was born to Serbian immigrants Nenad and Melanija Živojinović in Fernie, British Columbia. Like Lee's family, the Lifesons had their lives disrupted by World War II and sought refuge in the United States. The problem was that the land of the free didn't want them.

"They tried to get into the States, but they were denied and then sent to Canada," he told *Classic Rock* in 2016. "In cities like Toronto, they didn't really want these people, but Eastern Europeans could find work in the mines in British Columbia. . . . We eventually moved to Toronto in the early 50s because there were greater opportunities there."

Lee and Lifeson's family histories and exotic ethnicities made junior high school a socially daunting experience until they found one another at age 13. Once that happened, they were inseparable.

"We connected and we bonded," Lifeson told *Rolling Stone* in 2015. "We were friends in grade nine, for example, in a class of 30 kids, and we were not friends with anybody in that class, except the two of us. So we were outsiders, but not in that sense of being ostracized or shut out or something. We just kind of hung out, and we felt like everybody else was a jerk."

They also became more interested in playing music and less interested in showing up for school.

"We loved to learn all those great Cream songs, play along to the record player, and play them better and better and better," the guitarist said. "We were beginning to look at music more seriously and really trying to figure out what the musicians were playing, how the bands worked. And we loved to play. We just couldn't get away from it."

Like Lee, Lifeson had also picked up the guitar at age 12 but was never asked to put it down in favor of another instrument. In 1996, he told the publication *Guitar One* that he had always enjoyed music from an early age and was exposed to a wide range of genres growing up. When the British Invasion gave way to the Summer of Love in 1967, however, Lifeson decided it was time to commit his life to playing music. He cited such artists as Jimi Hendrix, the Jefferson Airplane, and the Grateful Dead as groups that profoundly affected him.

"From that point on, music became what I wanted to do with the rest of my life," he said.

He said that his first guitar was a present from his parents, who had paid the princely sum of $25 for it. He described it as a Kent classical guitar that used steel strings instead of the standard nylon. Although it left much to be desired, he learned his first riffs on it, which were "The Last Time" and "(I Can't Get No) Satisfaction" by the Rolling Stones.

Lifeson said that after Mick and Keef, he moved on to Jeff Beck's stint with the Yardbirds and to the superhuman guitar playing of Jimi Hendrix. The guitarist who had influenced him the most in his youth, however, was Jimmy Page of Led Zeppelin.

"He just blew me away," Lifeson said. "I wanted to play exactly like him!"

CLOCKWISE FROM LEFT Alex Lifeson and Neil Peart in Birmingham, England, on February 12, 1978. A little more than a week later, they would play a legendary concert in London where a journalist insinuated that they were Nazis.

Former Cream bassist Jack Bruce onstage with the supergroup West, Bruce, and Laing in 1970. Lee cited Bruce as a major influence on his "obnoxious" bass playing.

Alex Lifeson backstage with his Gibson ES-355 guitar on one of the band's countless and unending tours.

“THE FIRST TIME I EVER GOT HIGH WAS WITH ALEX; HE WAS JUST A TERRIFIC POTHEAD, AND A TERRIBLE INFLUENCE ON ME.”

GEDDY LEE
to *Classic Rock*, 2016

Alex Lifeson, Neil Peart, and Geddy Lee (L-R) are not at all high in this promotional photo from 1978. Especially Geddy.

Lifeson strangles his Les Paul in 1977, the better to coax otherworldly sonic outbursts hidden deep within it.

Before long, he began to be influenced by guitar players from the progressive rock movement, such as Steve Hackett of Genesis. He described Hackett's playing as "textural" and said it greatly affected how he thought of his role in Rush.

"His parts in the early Genesis music influenced me as far as the textures in this band," he said. "As a result, I always wanted my guitar presence in Rush to be quite broad and fill a lot of space in an interesting way."

Lifeson also credited studying classical guitar in 1972 with broadening and expanding his abilities. While his classical technique would make a few appearances on Rush records throughout the years, he said that the real benefit of the lessons was that they taught him the importance of keeping his chops up.

"I found that, if I practiced [classical pieces] for an hour or two a day, my fingers just felt amazing," he said. "I could play anything. That was the real benefit."

Although it didn't occur to Lee and Lifeson right away that they should form a band together, they played together all the time, both plugging into the bassist's amp. The pair even managed to secure some remuneration for their performances, although it did not come in the form of money.

"We played in coffee shops for food—chips and gravy," the guitarist said. "We'd play British blues—mostly Cream stuff from the *Fresh Cream* period. I would pretend I was Eric Clapton, Geddy would pretend he was Jack Bruce, and we'd play 'Spoonful' for twenty minutes."

The pair also found another thing in common—the devil's lettuce.

"The first time I ever got high was with Alex," Lee revealed to *Rolling Stone* in 2020. "He was just a terrific pothead, and a terrible influence on me."

Lifeson met drummer John Rutsey in high school, which led to the formation of Rush. The band played local bars relentlessly, and eventually Lifeson came to the same conclusion Lee did. He wanted to drop out of high school and pursue music full-time. His parents didn't take the news any better than Lee's mother.

We know this because an argument between Lifeson and his parents about this very topic was filmed for the documentary *Come on Children*, which depicted the lives of real teenagers, including one Alex Živojinović. In one clip from the documentary, he gets into a lively debate with his parents in which he tells them that the band can make $80 a night playing in Toronto bars, so what's the point of finishing high school? His parents, meanwhile, just want the sullen, fidgeting pothead to finish the twelfth grade.

At one point, his father says something that appears to be a joke gone awry. He tells his son that it's hard to support yourself even when you do everything right, as he knew from his own hardscrabble existence. As an aside, he throws in the statement, "Everything went wrong with him so far," and the room erupts with laughter.

One can see in young Alex's eyes that the words wounded him. In fairness to Nenad and Melanija, though, they're just trying to stop their kid, already a seventeen-year-old father, from throwing his life away on something that sure sounded like a stupid fantasy.

"I don't see why I have to go through all the bullshit of high school to learn music," Lifeson retorts. It's the exact thing no parent wants to hear out of their teenager.

The clip is fascinating, and it makes an appearance in the 2010 Rush documentary *Beyond the Lighted Stage*. In a 2012 essay about *Come on Children*, David Blakeslee of the *Criterion Cast* podcast wrote that it's an inspiring few minutes of video for anyone considering taking a risk in life when the voice of reason is rightly begging them not to.

"Those of us who ever took it upon ourselves to 'drop out' merely for the sake of dumping meaningless expectations imposed by others can look to Alex as a hero for defying the odds and proving the establishment wrong," he said.

Decades later, the guitarist told CBC Radio One's Tom Power that back then, he simply wasn't thinking about any of the real-world concerns that his family was trying to impress upon him and prepare him for. Even if they were correct and his music career was a failure, he wasn't worried about that either.

"I really had a belief in myself," he said. "If this music thing doesn't work out, well then I'll do something else. I'll work with my dad as a plumber's assistant or whatever. But I really believed that this was going to work out. I never worried about it in the early days."

Lifeson defied the odds and became the exception to the rule. Unlike countless guitar-playing teenagers who dropped out of school to become famous musicians, he actually went and became a famous musician—so his bratty impudence was rewarded.

Still, if there's anything like an "alas" to be found in Lifeson's career, it's that he remains a criminally underrated guitarist. The website *HowStuffWorks* ranked him at #2 in the article, "The 22 Most Underrated Guitarists of All Time," in which they characterized his playing as "out-of-this-world-level incredible." So, what gives?

"Alex Lifeson wrote some of the best riffs you'll ever hear, and they're absolutely infectious and addictive," Mark Urban wrote, adding that when you play in a band composed entirely of virtuosos, someone is bound to get overlooked in all the oohing and aahing. It's just too bad it had to be him.

"Lifeson's playing is some of the best in rock history," he said, perhaps trying to single-handedly give the guitarist all the accolades he got screwed out over the years. "His ability to bounce back and forth from different complex time signatures without missing a beat is unbelievable."

The guitar playing that Lifeson produced on *2112* showed him to be an artist well on his way to occupying a singular niche among the masses of guitar heroes who have come and gone. In 1996, he told *Guitar One* that while the band would achieve many great things since then, *2112* was the creative breakthrough that set the tone for the rest of their career.

"I think *2112* was the turning point for Rush in general, and that was the beginning of my original style," he said. "There's a lot of aggression and anger on that record, and I think, because it was written so much from the heart, it was where we began to develop a band signature."

Legendary jazz drummer Gene Krupa, a major influence on Neil Peart. The Rush drummer described Krupa as "the first rock drummer" for his flash and flamboyance.

III. NEIL PEART

Drummer Neil Peart was born on September 12, 1952, in Port Dalhousie in the Canadian province of Ontario. He entered Rush's orbit in July 1974 when original drummer John Rutsey parted ways with the band for health reasons after the release of their self-titled debut album.

Stylistically, his playing was as different from Rutsey's as it gets. Rutsey had been a basic backbeat drummer whose simple style was perfect for the band's first record—the only one in their entire catalog that could be classified as basic, meat-and-potatoes hard rock. As good as the debut is, Lee and Lifeson were already itching to move on from that style into a more progressive one; and Rutsey wasn't interested in pursuing that. It just didn't interest him.

Peart, meanwhile, was instantly receptive to playing the more adventurous music Lee and Lifeson wanted to create. He had taken up drums when he was thirteen years old, and by his own admission, everything else in his life permanently fell by the wayside at that point. All he wanted to do was play and play and play, and between that and his rabid creative curiosity, he was very much simpatico with the bassist and guitarist. He was the perfect drummer for the music Lee and Lifeson wanted to explore next.

"When I started playing, I played in R&B bands," Peart told *Rolling Stone* in 2015. "I played James Brown, Wilson Pickett, Otis Redding, and all that."

Eventually, Peart moved on to the same hard rock music that had inspired Lee and Lifeson, thanks in part to the deranged performances of the Who's Keith Moon. In 2003, he told *Zildjian.com* that he also took a lot of early inspiration from Mitch Mitchell of the Jimi Hendrix Experience, Michael Giles of King Crimson, and Bill Bruford of Yes. In 2015, he told NPR that as much as he had gushed over Moon and the like over the years, he traced it all back to Gene Krupa.

"He was the first rock drummer, in very many ways," he said. "He was the first drummer to command the spotlight and the first drummer to be celebrated for his solos, because they were very flamboyant."

Peart also brought something essential to the band. He could write lyrics, something no one else in Rush felt particularly compelled to do.

He didn't write in a typical rock style, so there were no references to "baby" or "mama" and nothing about how anyone had done him wrong. It was almost entirely influenced by literature, something no lyricist before or since has embraced to the degree Peart did. In 2015, he told *Rolling Stone* that it wasn't just because he liked big, pretty, multisyllabic words—rather, his lyrical choices made musical sense.

"Some of those formal phrasings were because I was very much driven by rhythm of words," he said. "A line will strike me just because of its drumming rhythm."

Peart found himself in a bit of a pickle with the press for extolling the virtues of Objectivist writer Ayn Rand in the gatefold of *2112*. The concept of the "2112" suite had some similarities to her 1938 novella *Anthem*, so in 1991, he told the radio show *Rockline* that to avoid looking like a plagiarist, he added a line to the credits that said, "With acknowledgment to the genius of Ayn Rand." He clarified that it was less about taking her literally, though, and more about taking inspiration from her individual-against-conformity point of view.

"That album came out of a time of turmoil for us, where a lot of people were trying to tell us what to do and how to commercialize our music," he said. "I think that sense of rebellion and the sense of repression that we felt from those around us came through the music And it has such a strong sincerity about it because we really did feel that way at the time, that it was us against the world."

Peart's lyrical prowess evolved as the years passed, and he was repeatedly recognized for his virtuosity on the kit. Fellow phenome-

Neil Peart bashes the skins during the *All the World's a Stage* tour, an endeavor that saw countless North American concert venues reduced to rubble by this humble Canadian three-piece.

RUSH
neil
RUSH
peart

nal drummer Stewart Copeland of the Police told *Rolling Stone* in 2015 that Peart—whom he described as "the most air-drummed-to drummer of all time"—was entirely deserving of every accolade that was ever thrown his way.

"Neil pushes that band, which has a lot of musicality, a lot of ideas crammed into every eight bars," Stewart Copeland said to *Rolling Stone* in 2020. "But he keeps the throb, which is the important thing. And he can do it while doing all kinds of cool shit."

In 1997, the drummer was blindsided by tragedy when his nineteen-year-old daughter Selena died in a car accident. Less than a year later, his wife Jacqueline Taylor died of cancer. In 2015, the famously agnostic drummer told *Rolling Stone* that at the time, he briefly blamed mystical forces for what had happened to his first wife and daughter.

"When something really shitty happens, of course immediately you look to why," he said. "I went all supernatural: 'Somebody must have put a curse on me, I must have done something really horrible, God must be mad at me.' I had to sift through all of that shit again looking for meaning."

After over a year of grieving on a solo motorcycle journey that took him through North and South America, he returned to the band, which had gone on an indefinite hiatus. In 2000, he married photographer Carrie Nuttall; and a decade later, they had a daughter named Olivia. The band remained active until the *R40* tour in 2015, at which point Peart devoted himself to his family life full-time.

Sadly, he didn't get to enjoy it for long. Not long after coming off the road, he was diagnosed with glioblastoma, a highly aggressive form of brain cancer. He lived with it for over three years and let only a small handful of people know, such as his family, bandmates, and a few other close associates. He had asked them all to keep it a secret, which they did until three days after he passed on January 7, 2020.

When it was announced, musicians from every genre weighed in with comments about what he had meant to them, how much he had meant to them, and how much they had been inspired by him.

"It absolutely breaks my heart to pieces to get the news of the passing of one of my greatest heroes of all time," said Dream Theater drummer Mike Portnoy on his Instagram page. "Neil Peart will always be a mentor and a hero to me and his influence on me as a drummer for the past 40 years is absolutely impossible to measure."

It's been said before, but it bears repeating: Neil Peart was the greatest drummer who ever lived, and Rush would not have become the band they became without him. Furthermore, the idea of replacing him is daunting.

He was the youngest drummer ever to be inducted into the *Modern Drummer* Readers Poll Hall of Fame at thirty, so on a technical level, very few people could match him. And of those who could match him, were they also big readers who could craft the same type of lyric as Peart? Absolutely not.

Since his passing, fondness for him and his work has not diminished; and in the Internet age, he arguably has more reach and influence than he ever did before. In fact, there's a persuasive argument to be made that he's more popular now than ever, since Spotify and YouTube are affording his music unlimited free access to new generations of listeners, and they just keep getting born every day. In that sense, he joins a pantheon of musicians like Freddie Mercury, Jimi Hendrix, and John Lennon. Their lives were cut short, but the music was too good for anyone to leave it at that.

"NEIL PUSHES THAT BAND, WHICH HAS A LOT OF MUSICALITY, A LOT OF IDEAS CRAMMED INTO EVERY EIGHT BARS. BUT HE KEEPS THE THROB, WHICH IS THE IMPORTANT THING. AND HE CAN DO THAT WHILE DOING ALL KINDS OF COOL SHIT."

STEWART COPELAND
to *Rolling Stone*, 2015

Pepe's
CAFE & GRILL

AN EASYGOING RELATIONSHIP

3

TERRY BROWN WAS BORN ON JUNE 2, 1947, in Watford, a town in the English county of Hertfordshire. As a young man in the 1960s, he moved to London to get into the field of studio engineering and looked for opportunities to get a foot in the door.

There were several independent music studios where he could pursue his interests, gain experience, and ply his trade. The British pop music scene was growing, ground-breaking records were being made, and he could get in on the ground floor.

Soon enough, he was working in the legendary Olympic Studios, where the Rolling Stones had recorded their debut LP. Here, he met studio engineer Keith Grant, whom he described on his official website as "a great teacher." He learned the science of how to set up a studio while working on sessions for such artists as the Moody Blues, the Spencer Davis Group, and Donovan.

At one point, Brown worked with the Jimi Hendrix Experience as they recorded the 1967 album *Axis: Bold as Love*. It was just for one evening, as the opening track "EXP" was being created; but Brown said the nature of the recording made it a challenge.

"Jimi had a double Marshall stack, then strapped to the side of it was this long, thin, four-foot horn," he said. "Trying to mic it was a bit of a challenge. But he was such a lovely guy, it didn't matter what he did. He just wanted to make it as good as possible."

He said that Procol Harum producer Denny Cordell was another valuable mentor. The two worked on the band's self-titled 1967 debut album, which he described as a transformative experience.

"I learned so much from Denny Cordell, as far as how to listen and how to be patient," he said. "A band would start playing in the middle of the afternoon, and then by the early evening, the same tune had a maturity to it that we hadn't heard three or four hours before, just by nurturing the performances and listening carefully. It was really a fascinating experience. I loved it. I learned a lot from him."

In the early 1970s, Brown left London for Toronto to open Toronto Sound, the first sixteen-track recording studio in Canada's history. On a previous trip, he got a sense of the city's local music scene, which was still small but showed potential—it was vibrant, and there was a palpable buzz in the air.

The Jimi Hendrix Experience influenced Rush in their early bar band days. Hendrix was also the subject of a recording session early in co-producer Terry Brown's career.

PREVIOUS Rush in 1978 with their "fourth man," co-producer Terry Brown, who fondly recalled *2112* as "a lot of fun to make."

There was also opportunity. Toronto was not yet full of state-of-the-art recording facilities like London, so anyone opening a new one might find their business quite popular with local musicians before too long. It was also here that he intended to more seriously pursue work as a record producer.

Before he could start, he received a call from one Vic Wilson, who co-managed Rush along with Ray Danniels. They had recorded tracks for their self-financed debut album but weren't pleased with the results. Could this British producer, who was by now establishing himself as a real presence in Toronto, help bring it up to code?

"The boys had been recording at a studio downtown during the graveyard shift," he said. "They were getting a great deal on time by going in late at night and working 'til the wee hours of the morning. They got some great stuff recorded, but they were having trouble finishing it off, putting the icing on the cake, so to speak. So management called me and said they wanted to bring the band in and finish the album off."

He said that the album was mixed in three days. In 2021, he told *Classic Rock* that those sessions had gone so well that the band decided he was the right person to work with on their next projects.

"We had such a good time, they asked me to get involved on a long-term basis," he said. From then on, Rush and Terry Brown continued to collaborate, eventually creating nine consecutive studio albums—*Rush* (1974) to *Signals* (1982)—a rare feat in rock history.

He and the trio parted ways after *Signals*, and Brown went on to work with a wide variety of artists across multiple genres. One of his more high-profile co-production efforts was with the band Cutting Crew, whose 1986 studio album *Broadcast* featured the hit single "(I Just) Died in Your Arms," a global hit that topped the charts in numerous countries, including the United States.

Brown also co-produced three albums by the progressive metal band Fates Warning, including 1991's *Parallels*, which many die-hard fans consider one of the group's finest. He also worked on the band's *A Pleasant Shade of Grey*, which gives the "2112" suite a run for its money by consisting entirely of a single, fifty-four-minute song. They wussed out and indexed all the movements into separate tracks on the compact disc, which some may consider cheating. At the same time, no vinyl album can accommodate fifty-four minutes on a single side, so it was always fated to be chopped in half at the very least.

He also earned additional street cred when he worked with Metal Blade Records recording artists Lizzy Borden on their 1989 album *Mas-*

Co-producer Terry Brown's unusually fertile run of nine studio records with Rush started when he came in to finish off their 1974 debut and kept going until 1982's *Signals*.

ter of Disguise. Finally, he produced what was, without question, the greatest album of 1991: the tragically misunderstood *Angel Rat* by Voivod, which was one thousand times better than *Metallica* and ten billion times better than *Nevermind*. Again, these are scientific facts.

Decades later, even after amassing a résumé that anyone would be proud of, he still recalls the few weeks working with Rush on *2112* as one of his fondest experiences. It was a joy from start to finish, because he was working on music he loved, right down to the first time he heard it.

"They played me the material," he said. "I loved it. I was a huge fan of the band at that point. I'm still a huge fan of the band, but my enthusiasm was growing, and when I heard the material, I just loved it. And we just got down to it."

"Terry was always quite involved in the whole aspect of putting together a Rush record," Lifeson told *Guitar Shop* in 1999. "Besides being the co-producer, he was often involved in the latter stages of arrangements."

Rush was fiercely protective of their creative vision, so it might sound strange that they would allow anybody into the trenches with them while making a record. Brown said they were absolutely committed to achieving their artistic vision, but they welcomed his input and treated him like a real collaborator. If anything, he remembered the experience as being a lot of fun.

"There was a lot of spontaneity, to be honest with you," he said. "We would make decisions on the fly about, 'Maybe take a few bars out of this verse,' or, 'Let's move the bridge forward.' Lots of stuff like that, just in terms of arrangement and production ideas."

Brown's approach in the studio facilitated this. Bluntly, he was not an angry, tyrannical jerk who made recording sessions toxic and horrible; nor was he a Phil Spector–type producer who ran recording sessions with an iron fist. With Terry Brown, Rush never experienced a screaming lunatic who hurled projectiles at his clients and brandished firearms in the name of "motivation." He would not ask for fifty-seven takes of anything.

"That's not my style," he said.

He added that he even asked for additional takes in a manner so civil and respectful that it was hard for anyone to refuse him. Rush, whom he frequently referred to as "the boys," became so used to hearing the carefully worded request from him that it became something of a comedy bit between them.

"That was really good, guys," he would say. "Can we just do one more?"

It was an effective way of getting another good take out of them, possibly a better one. After a while, the statement even became "a standing joke" between the band and the producer. On occasion, he might have to be more insistent; but it was all in the name of getting the right performance.

"I definitely would insist on doing another take if I felt the band could do a better take," he said. "From that standpoint, I was pretty adamant. But other than that, it was much more of an easygoing relationship in terms of recording."

Alex Lifeson uses seductive and hypnotic eye contact to mesmerize onlookers backstage at Bakersfield, California's Civic Auditorium on September 26, 1977.

PROOF OF CONCEPT

4

999 QUEEN STREET

Rush formed in 1968, and according to guitarist Alex Lifeson, the name came courtesy of original drummer John Rutsey's brother. The drummer and the guitarist were in a band called the Projection, and Bill Rutsey thought they could do better.

"John's brother Bill had said, 'You need a better name for the band—how about Rush?'" the guitarist told *Classic Rock* in 2016. "And we liked it."

The lineup fluctuated several times over the next few years, sometimes including a fourth member. In 1969, bassist and vocalist Geddy Lee found himself on the outs with the group. For the first and only time in their history, he was fired, albeit in a roundabout way that consisted of the whole band breaking up and then reforming minus Lee under a different name.

For decades, the story went that the ouster took place at the behest of manager Ray Danniels. In Lee's 2023 memoir *My Effin' Life*, he exonerated the wrongly accused manager and revealed that Rutsey had been the culprit all along. Their drummer wanted "someone hipper," and while guitarist Alex Lifeson didn't necessarily feel the same way, he passively acquiesced to the drummer's wishes. One could say he had chosen not to decide.

That situation didn't last long, and Lee eventually returned to the group. Indeed, if one consults the *I Ching*—an ancient Chinese divination text that functions as a guide to an ethical life—and respects its principles, one understands that the situation had created an energy imbalance and nature swooped in to correct it, solidifying the lineup around Lee, Lifeson, and Rutsey. If there were any hard feelings, they were lost in the

“THE BARS WOULDN’T HIRE A BAND THAT JUST PLAYED THEIR OWN SHITTY SONGS, AND OUR SONGS WERE PRETTY SHITTY BACK THEN!”

GEDDY LEE
to *Classic Rock*, 2016

Pleased to meet you, hope you guessed their names. Rush backstage at the Civic Auditorium in Bakersfield, California, on September 26, 1977.

PREVIOUS On stage in 1977, Geddy Lee manifests a facial expression that recalls Iron Maiden's Rush-influenced bassist, Steve Harris.

deluge of politeness and civility that characterizes the Great White North. Sadly, that newfound stability wouldn't last forever, either.

They endured the false starts, lineup changes, and style changes that plague most bands in their formative years. They also performed at their fair share of venues where they had no business being in the first place, such as at 999 Queen Street in Toronto. Rush's first roadie, Ian Grandy, told *Guitar International* in 2009 that this unique venue was, in fact, an active and populated insane asylum. They played there as part of paying their dues—literally.

"The guys belonged to the musicians' union, and there was an older guard of people who ran the union and its elections," Grandy said. "The guys who held the key to the ballot box and counted the votes were also the guys running for office, which kind of stunk."

Grandy said the musicians' union had drawn battle lines between the old guard and the young, hairy rock dudes. Rush fell firmly into the latter camp. The union had the power to dole out gigs to musicians, and Grandy said that the psychiatric hospital concert was intended to chasten the young whippersnappers. Ever the consummate

ABOVE Alex Lifeson rips a power chord at the Aragon Ballroom in Chicago on January 7, 1978.

RIGHT Geddy Lee in the studio with a quite large synthesizer boasting a great many knobs, dials, and other controllers to get those cosmic, intergalactic, musical saw type of sounds.

professionals, they set up and started playing anyway, although it's hard to say if anyone in the audience enjoyed it.

"[There] were about seven old ladies who they put right in front of the P.A. speakers, and they sat there unblinking and almost catatonic, and seemed totally unaware," Grandy said. "I couldn't help thinking that these were probably somebody's mom, and what a sad way to end up."

Undeterred, the band kept playing at clubs and bars, slowly and methodically building a following. While they eventually started writing their own material, they had to keep psychedelic cover songs by Cream and Blue Cheer in their repertoire alongside their own material. It was for one simple reason.

"The bars wouldn't hire a band that just played their own shitty songs," Lee said to *Classic Rock* in 2016, "and our songs were pretty shitty back then!"

The Lee-Lifeson-Rutsey incarnation of the group would go on to record their first single in 1973 and their self-titled debut album the following year. The lineup would change again soon after, but once that happened, the group stayed as it was for the next forty-one years and would eventually craft seminal rock albums that are still getting played this very minute, even as you read this.

RUSH (1974)

Rush's self-titled debut came out in 1974, and when it did, they were complete unknowns outside of the Toronto bar circuit. That changed when Donna Halper, program director for the WMMS radio station in Cleveland, got "Working Man" played on the air. The positive listener response was massive, giving the group their first big break. Halper said she knew the song might strike a chord with Cleveland radio listeners.

"I was constantly looking for great records for Cleveland," Halper said. "As a music director, you want to find those certain unique things, and in the case of Cleveland in 1974, it was still a working-class town . . . the urban renewal that we see today didn't exist back then. Back then, Republic Steel lit the sky orange with pollution every night."

Her initial hunch that the record would be well received in Cleveland was correct, but it didn't stay a regional secret for long. Word spread, airplay increased, and touring got underway because listeners across North America loved "Working Man," whose riffs are as heavy as its lyrics are relatable.

Rush is a record full of strong tracks, although it should be said that "Take a Friend" is not one of them. It must also be noted that the lyrics, which Lee and Lifeson hastily penned during the recording sessions, score a C minus at their absolute best. Having said that, songs like "Finding My Way," "What You're Doing," and "Here Again" are so good that the positives vastly outweigh the negatives. Overall, a solid hard rock debut album with great performances.

Lifeson and Lee during the *All the World's a Stage* tour. Despite the complexity of the music, they always seemed to have a blast onstage, and the camaraderie they enjoyed since their school days is easy to see.

FLY BY NIGHT (1975)

After the debut's release, original drummer John Rutsey left the group and was replaced by Neil Peart. Rush went on tour to promote the debut, and the sudden whirlwind of activity required some adjustment for the young band.

"There's a very famous picture everyone has seen when they finally did get signed to Mercury Records and Neil had just joined the band," Halper said. "The guys take a picture for the trade publications, which you did back then in that pre-Internet era, and they do not look happy. But it wasn't that they weren't happy, it's that they were exhausted."

After coming off the road to promote the debut album, they returned to Toronto Sound to begin work on their second record, *Fly by Night*. It was the first to feature their new drummer and lyricist, and he forcefully announces his presence all over the opening track, "Anthem." The song shares its name with the 1938 Ayn Rand novella, and while it doesn't detail the story's events, its lyrics express Objectivist principles with the line, "It was for me, not you, I came to write this song."

The song opens the record, and from the second the needle drops, a completely transformed band emerges from the vinyl. Between the elevation of the musicianship and the radically different approach to the lyrics, Peart completely transformed Rush; and Halper had been eager to hear his impact on the band.

"I was excited as a music director to hear how Neil's influence was going to manifest itself," Halper said. "I started hearing elements of that."

The album features what amounts to early prototypes of Rush trademarks. "By-Tor and the Snow Dog" is the earliest example of the band dabbling in epic tracks broken up into movements, and "Rivendell" shows the band getting into lyrics with fantasy themes. And who knows? Maybe it even inspired some people to crack open a book for once in their lives.

Meanwhile, "Making Memories" is an easy, breezy tune about life on the road with instrumentation that recalls side two of *Led Zeppelin III*. The title track is compact, bittersweet, and over much too soon at less than three and a half minutes.

Everything on *Fly by Night*—from the songwriting to the performances to the production—represented a big step forward from the debut. The title track even stood a chance of getting airplay.

"I thought *Fly by Night* was a very nice transition into their new direction," Halper said. "There are touches of it that are very reminiscent of the first, and then there's stuff on it that is completely unique and different."

One aspect of producing another commercial rock record that had *not* improved was the rock press's attitude toward the band. Critical resistance to the band was only strengthening and becoming more combative, intense, and hard to ignore.

"The *New York Times* and *Rolling Stone* were relentlessly brutal in their critiques of Rush," Halper said. "Their critics could not find a good thing to say about the band at all, under any circumstances."

While it's different strokes for different folks and no accounting for taste and all that, it is nevertheless challenging to pinpoint an exact reason for the acidic vitriol toward the band from a pantheon of rock critics. Perhaps some were symbolically bemoaning that rock music was moving on from the 1960s and into something that had nothing to do with hippie culture; one might also opine that the critics were ornery because they used to be with it, but then they changed what "it" was. The zeitgeist is nothing if not ephemeral.

"I think that in many cases this is like, 'Music was better in the old days,'" Halper proposed. "'Nothing good has happened since the Rolling Stones and the Beatles.'"

Terry Brown, meanwhile, felt precisely the opposite. In fact, in 2021, he said in *Classic Rock* that he was aware of all the criticisms and utterly dismissive of all of them.

"I always thought they were great," he said. "I thought they were new and exciting. I didn't buy into the Led Zeppelin thing, to be honest. I just thought they were great players and characters, and very talented. I remember Alex being an amazing player, doubling his parts. That was a big feature for me at the time. And Ged's voice was astonishing."

CARESS OF STEEL (1975)

Despite failing to win over the rock press, the band were now ascendant in their trajectory. *Fly by Night* won over new fans, sold a respectable number of copies, and moved the band another step forward. They believed their next record, *Caress of Steel*, would be an even bigger success; and on October 10, 1975, the *St. Catharines Standard* agreed.

"Rush's last album, *Fly by Night*, sold 110,000 copies and made the top 100 in *Billboard*," the publication said. "The band's new album, *Caress of Steel*, was just released last week and from all indication looks more promising financially."

Sadly, the publication erred in its assessment. *Caress of Steel* sold fewer copies than its predecessor, the most egregious crime one can commit in the music industry. This is unfortunate because the album is more musically adventurous than *Fly by Night* and shows a band with a lot of fire in the belly for exploring new ideas, especially progressive ones.

It starts with "Bastille Day," a magnificently aggressive choice to kick off the festivities. The song is a four-and-a-half-minute history lesson about the French Revolution, and frankly, one wonders if anyone who heard it even bothered to read the lyrics. After the throwaway "I Think I'm Going Bald" and the wistful "Lakeside Park" comes "The Necromancer"—in three movements spanning twelve-and-a-half minutes.

The band's next attempt at an epic (in the style of "By-Tor and the Snow Dog"), this extended track constitutes a refinement and elevation of the material from *Fly by Night*. The use of dynamics is also leaps and bounds beyond what the band were doing on the previous album. But perhaps most importantly, the second movement, "Under the Shadow," features an utterly unhinged jam section that makes them sound like they're trying to be the next Cream.

The final song on the album is "The Fountain of Lamneth." It is their first attempt at a suite taking up an entire album side, and it demonstrates their ambition to stretch out into more progressive territory. However, if it was an attempt to have a "Close to the Edge" or "Supper's Ready," that's going to be a "no." The execution is flawless, but the ideas aren't there.

Album sales were disappointing, and numerous tour dates drew sparse crowds. From a

What's wrong with this picture of Neil Peart backstage at the Gaumont in England on May 13, 1979? 1) He's smiling, and 2) he's not reading a book.

Geddy Lee at Le Studio in Morin Heights, Quebec, where the band recorded their last three albums with co-producer Terry Brown.

business perspective, it was hard to say Rush had created proof of concept for their own existence.

Halper, meanwhile, had left WMMS for New York City, where she had been hired to be East Coast Director of Artists and Repertoire at Mercury Records, Rush's label. She said that they had clear expectations for her.

"They were expecting me to find the next Rush," she said. "The president of Mercury, Irwin Steinberg, was really eager to build out the talent scouts that they had and hire more of them. Since I had discovered Rush, they brought me to New York and basically wanted me to discover another Rush."

She said the label was having a hard time getting the band airplay. They wanted the band to record something that could reach the top 40, and *Caress of Steel* was not it.

"Nobody at Mercury knew what to do with it," Halper said. "It's like, 'How do you promote this?' They were really hoping for a top 40 single . . . and instead you've got the 12-minute tracks. I have the feeling that people at the label were mystified by it, and they didn't know how to promote it. . . . The record sold very poorly," she said. "It didn't get a lot of airplay for the same exact reasons—people just didn't quite know what to do with it."

PANACEA

Caress of Steel was a sluggish seller and didn't receive Gold certification from the Recording Industry Association of America until 1993, eighteen years later.

Halper also said that she believed Rush released this album too early in their career. It was

What comes from Toronto and has six arms and seven necks? Rush onstage during the *All the World's a Stage* tour.

an adventurous record, and it may have been better received if they had been more established than in 1975.

"I think if this had come out as their fifth or sixth record, it might have done better," she said. "If it came out after Rush had established itself and people had really fallen in love with their first three or four records, then you can go off the beaten path and do something a little bit strange or different. But I think they did it a little too soon."

Lifeson conceded a similar point in the liner notes to the *2112* 40th Anniversary Edition.

"It was a difficult record for a lot of people to take and maybe a difficult one for a band at our stage," he said. He still made no apologies for the band trying to think bigger than they had on *Fly by Night*, and he said it was an essential step in the band's overall artistic approach.

"For us, it was really important to exercise our songwriting and arranging skills," he said. "We really felt like we were taking some chances and growing and going somewhere. . . . We really loved that record."

In Rush lore, Mercury Records is said to have wanted to clamp down on the band and stifle their creativity. It's undoubtedly true that the label wanted the band to do something they didn't want to, and it was for commercial reasons. Halper later stressed that many factors were at play, including the record label's resources.

"Mercury Records at that time was a smaller label," Halper said. "The pressure was on all of their acts. 'If we signed you, we want to recoup what we've given you. We gave these guys an advance. We spent money on promoting these guys. Where's the hit single?' In the case of Bachman-Turner Overdrive, they were having tons of hit singles, so that's what the expectation was."

Halper also stressed that Rush didn't receive special treatment or were singled out by the label; instead, Mercury Records wanted every act to have hit singles—and Rush just happened to be one band of many. She stressed that, despite the popular legend of Mercury Records being big meanies who wanted to neuter Rush artistically, the truth simply had more to do with how the music business operated back then.

"I remember those conversations, and it wasn't just about Rush," she said. "I remember those conversations about lots of bands, because back in those days, getting a hit single was crucial."

Despite the legitimate market concerns, the story of Rush taking on their label à la David and Goliath has taken on mythical status, with Mercury Records cast in an antagonistic light, relishing the role of the Philistine giant of Gath.

"That's not how it was at all," Halper said.

She said that the people at Mercury Records were well intended and not looking to toss the Canadian threesome into a gulag for making weird music. There was simply one overriding question that eclipsed all other considerations.

"I have the memos from A&R meetings," she said. "Relentlessly, the question was, 'Does this band have a hit single? Does this band have a hit single? What's the hit single?' That was a constant, so the fact that Rush didn't have one was quite an object of consternation for the people at the label. But again, let me repeat, it wasn't just Rush."

She said that even fearsome Casablanca recording artists KISS had to play ball in this sense. Their concerts may have been pyrotech-

Marshall

BELOW Alex Lifeson annihilates the fretboard at the Aragon Ballroom in Chicago on January 7, 1978.

RIGHT Lee-Lifeson-Peart in Cleveland on December 17, 1977. That night they would perform at the city's Public Auditorium, where their sonic onslaught destroyed everything in its path, leaving only the memory of the concert in its wake.

nic events that pulled out all the stops and gave everyone in every seat their money's worth, but did they have a hit single? "Beth," which was only intended to be a B-side, famously blew up when it was played on the radio instead of the A-side, and it changed the band's fortunes dramatically.

"There were certain bands whose entire album was completely different from this one cut," she said. "It would get the fans really angry, because the fans that liked the top 40 single would buy the record expecting that it would be all like that, and none of it was like that."

Halper said that the band's relationship with Mercury was never adversarial, and they were grateful to be with the label. At the same time, they weren't sure the label understood what they were doing, although there were exceptions, such as A&R executive Cliff Burnstein, who went on to co-found Metallica's management company, Q Prime.

"They loved Cliff Burnstein," she said. "They got along fine with the people at the label, but they never really felt like the people at the label understood them the way Cliff and I did."

Halper remembered others from Mercury who were really trying to do right by Rush. She specifically mentioned Head of Publicity Sheryl Feuerstein.

"She tried real hard to publicize the band," Halper said.

She added that at one point, she conducted market research to demonstrate the viability of recording artists who never scored a hit single, also known as album rock artists.

"I wrote a memo about Black Sabbath and Genesis," she said. "I'm trying to come up with an explanation for how these bands are popular and to tell them not to give up on Rush. They were still coming from that attitude of, 'A band cannot be a success without a hit single.' That's how the record companies looked at it, and anybody that tells you different wasn't there."

Terry Brown, who had now worked on all three albums with Rush, still stands behind *Caress of Steel*. He does, however, acknowledge a few minor flaws that he would love to go back and fix if he could.

"It could use a little bit more refining, there's no doubt about it," he said. "I actually wouldn't mind having a crack at remixing that record. I think that would be kind of fun to do. I'll have to run that by the record label at some point, or by the guys, more to the point, and see what their reaction would be."

Caress of Steel will likely always be a dark horse in the Rush catalog, and it's true that the side-long epic "The Fountain of Lamneth" had some room for improvement. And while spoilers are bad and disclosing them is wrong, it doesn't give away too much to say they would get it right the next time. Meanwhile, Lifeson noted as far back as a 1980 interview with *Guitar Player* that their much-maligned third record was pivotal to their career and made possible everything that followed.

"*Caress of Steel* wasn't a very commercial album," he said. "Yet for us, it was a very successful album in terms of our own sense of creativity. We tried doing a number of things differently on the LP—longer songs, different melodic things—and it was a stepping stone for us. Without *Caress of Steel*, we couldn't have done *2112*."

ALIGNMENT

5

WHEN RUSH ENTERED TORONTO SOUND to record their follow-up to *Caress of Steel*, they were in a fragile state. They had been on the road since August 1975, beginning with a string of Canadian dates on August 24, 1975, in Lansdowne Park, Ottawa. Playing nearly seventy concerts over four months, they wrapped up the tour on January 10, 1976.

Rush had not been booed offstage, nor had they suffered any other spectacular indignity at the hands of concertgoers. Instead, they said the shows were meagerly attended and audiences had difficulty with the dense material from *Caress of Steel*. Much of the reception ranged from lukewarm to indifferent, which, when sustained over a period of months, just gets to you after a while.

A hostile reception from an angry crowd can at least make a good story to laugh over years later and, in some cases, might even serve as a badge of honor (hell, the Stooges made an entire career out of it). Indifference, though, was a different story. There was no cathartic rage to show that the band had at least made an impression, even a negative one. Instead, the muted response to the tour had the effect of slow, steady, increasing disappointment that enveloped the members. Between that and the label's quest for a hit single, a lot was riding on the next album.

Terry Brown was not really aware at the time that the band was in a bit of a rough spot. It's not that he wasn't paying attention; it was that Toronto Sound had taken off and he was busy cultivating a dream of his own. The reality was that it commanded his undivided attention when the band was touring to promote *Caress of Steel*.

Neil Peart gives the exotic percussion behind him some love at London's Hammersmith Odeon on February 20, 1978. Peart was different from most rock drummers in that he actually used his entire kit and none of it was for show.

PREVIOUS Geddy Lee during soundcheck at Bingley Hall in Staffordshire, England, on September 21, 1979.

"The band had gone through quite a lot of angst over the success, or lack thereof, of *Caress of Steel*, but I wasn't really aware of that," the producer said. "I was running a studio. I had clients coming in all the time, working 24/7, and I didn't really stay in touch with the boys when they were on the road. So when they arrived to do *2112*, we were starting on a whole new project."

Although the circumstances surrounding the band may have changed over the course of three albums, when it came time to begin production on *2112*, Brown said he and the band had already developed a standard operating procedure. *2112* would receive the same treatment.

"At that point, I had entered into an arrangement with management to co-produce, and the band would just show up, and it was like, 'Okay, what are we doing guys?'" he said. "They'd say, 'Well, we've got some ideas,' and they would play some stuff, and off we started in pre-production. Then, fast forward to *2112*, it wasn't really a lot different."

Much of the material for *2112* had been written during the *Caress of Steel* tour, in a venue's dressing room, in a hotel after the concert, even in the van that took them from city to city. Lifeson said he could remember that "The Temples of Syrinx" took shape in a Sault Ste. Marie dressing room.

Co-manager Ray Danniels had been dispatched to Mercury Records to regale all present with tales of what a hit-laden and commercial record their latest effort was shaping up to be. Lifeson said this was subterfuge in action. Danniels had not heard one note of the new material, either as it was being written or as it was being recorded. The guitarist said that every bit of that was on purpose.

"Ray was absolutely excluded," he said. "We never wanted him to know what we were doing or hear anything. It was better if we left it to the very end when it was finished. Then we would take it and we would play it for him and then he'd try to figure out what he had do with it."

Even though the band always showed up well prepared to make a new record, Brown said that, contrary to popular opinion, the three musicians were not absolutely 100 percent locked into completely finished arrangements from which there could be no deviation. Instead, he said it was exactly the opposite, and "the boys" were always eager to get his spontaneous input. It was a true collaboration and a genuine co-production.

"We'd make changes on the fly and bring things up to where they needed to be if they were lacking," he said. "The band already had ideas and things they wanted to do, and it was really a question of fine-tuning it with sounds and production ideas. We fine-tuned it into what you have been used to listening to."

There was one area in which Brown was completely hands-off: the lyrics. He said that Peart's lyrics for *2112* were a done deal by the time they entered the studio, and that had mostly been the case throughout their working relationship.

"The thing was, his lyrics were profound," Brown said. "He was an amazing drummer, but his writing was exemplary. He always had such interesting things to write about, and he wrote in such a succinct way that I didn't have to sit down and vet his lyrics. It was perfect. It never even occurred to me to do that."

He also clarified that Rush was, for the most part, the only band he worked with that never needed him to address lyric writing. It simply never came up, and he could not say the same about the vast majority of other artists he collaborated with over the years.

"With other artists I worked with, sometimes I would make some dramatic changes in the lyrics, in the way that the lyrics flowed, grammatical errors, and all kinds of stuff," he said, not naming names. "With Neil, I wouldn't. The only time I discussed something with him, I think I made an error, and he put me straight very quickly."

Hugh Syme, who designed the album jackets for every Rush studio album from *Caress of Steel* forward, co-signed on Brown's version of events. The illustrator loved Peart dearly, saying of him, "big brain, big drums, big heart." He also said the drummer was not above calling attention to grammar and syntax and would not hesitate to address any spelling errors a correspondent might make. You heard that right—Neil Peart would correct your spelling, which is probably the most Neil Peart thing that could possibly happen.

"There would be a lot of times I would get Neil's hand-drawn lyrics," Syme said. "He would send those to me, and he would also send a letter to go along with it. There would be a proper salutation, a date, and a place, depending on where he was writing from. It could be from a

Alex Lifeson, camouflaged at the Birmingham Odeon, gives his guitar some backstage TLC during the *A Farewell to Kings* tour.

"ALL I WAS INTERESTED IN WAS MAKING A GREAT RECORD."

TERRY BROWN to author, 2024.

hotel on the road, or it could be from his place in Montreal. It was all very formal. There was always indentation, paragraphs, and a formality, just because he was the wordsmith he was."

Syme added that if you had the good manners to write him back in a timely fashion, like you're supposed to, this courtesy could be fraught with terror for the correspondent who didn't regularly consult a dictionary.

"He edited himself judiciously, whereas sometimes I might be in a bit of a hurry," he said, detailing the dire consequences that would befall those who had not consulted their Funk & Wagnalls. "He would highlight a sentence, and say, 'Do you want to talk about this?' You know, talk about a dangling participle or a grammatical error. It was always in jest. It was always fun."

One time, Syme made the unforgivable error of returning a correspondence that referred to "waiting with bated breath," which he had unfortunately spelled with an "I" as in "B-A-I-T-E-D."

"Then he came back to me and said, "Dear sir, are we fishing or are we anticipating?" Syme said. "He never let a grammatical one go, you know? It was always in jest; it was all an intellectual kind of banter and challenge we set for each other."

Syme also got the opportunity to perform on *2112*. A keyboard player with Rush's label mates, the Ian Thomas Band, he was in the studio during the recording of *2112*; and Brown suggested that he play on the record. This kind of spontaneous attitude did not extend to anyone from the label, who mostly stayed out of it despite wanting a hit single.

"No A&R people came into the studio," Syme said. "I think the band was grateful for that, because they were on Mercury in the U.S. and they weren't flying in to micromanage their albums. As a band, they had their own vision, and they wouldn't have taken kindly to someone coming in and saying, 'What about this?' You know, they just wouldn't have. I think it's fair to say most musicians like to control their own sound."

Terry Brown said that even though spontaneous ideas were more than welcome during the recording process, the band usually knew what they wanted and showed up ready to do it. He appreciated the musicians' preparedness as much as their receptivity to outside ideas.

"The whole '2112' overture and everything was all written and decided and played," he said. "They'd rehearsed it, they had it together. But we made subtle changes . . . when you get into the production of an album, subtle changes make a lot of difference."

While much has been made of Rush's precarious position with Mercury Records after *Caress of Steel*, Brown said those pressures and considerations didn't intrude on the making of *2112*. The

Lifeson and Lee onstage in 1978, somewhere deep in the vastness of the Solar Federation.

music industry, promotional considerations, A&R, and all the other business hassles were checked at the door of Toronto Sound. The band and their co-producer focused on the music and didn't concern themselves with anything else. Conveniently, Brown was also a science fiction fan at the time.

"All I was interested in was making a great record," he said. "But I was immersed in this whole idea of other civilizations existing outside of our universe, and I was thrilled to bits. It was exciting. So it was the perfect record for me to be making at that point."

Once the album was recorded and "in the can," Syme said it was the first time he really grasped what a tightly knit unit Rush and Brown were. Not just anybody got to participate in making those records.

"When Terry asked me to come up to the studio to talk about album covers, and we ended up doing some tracks together on *2112*, I didn't realize then how militantly guarded their inner sanctum was as a band," the illustrator said. "I only later found out that was a privilege."

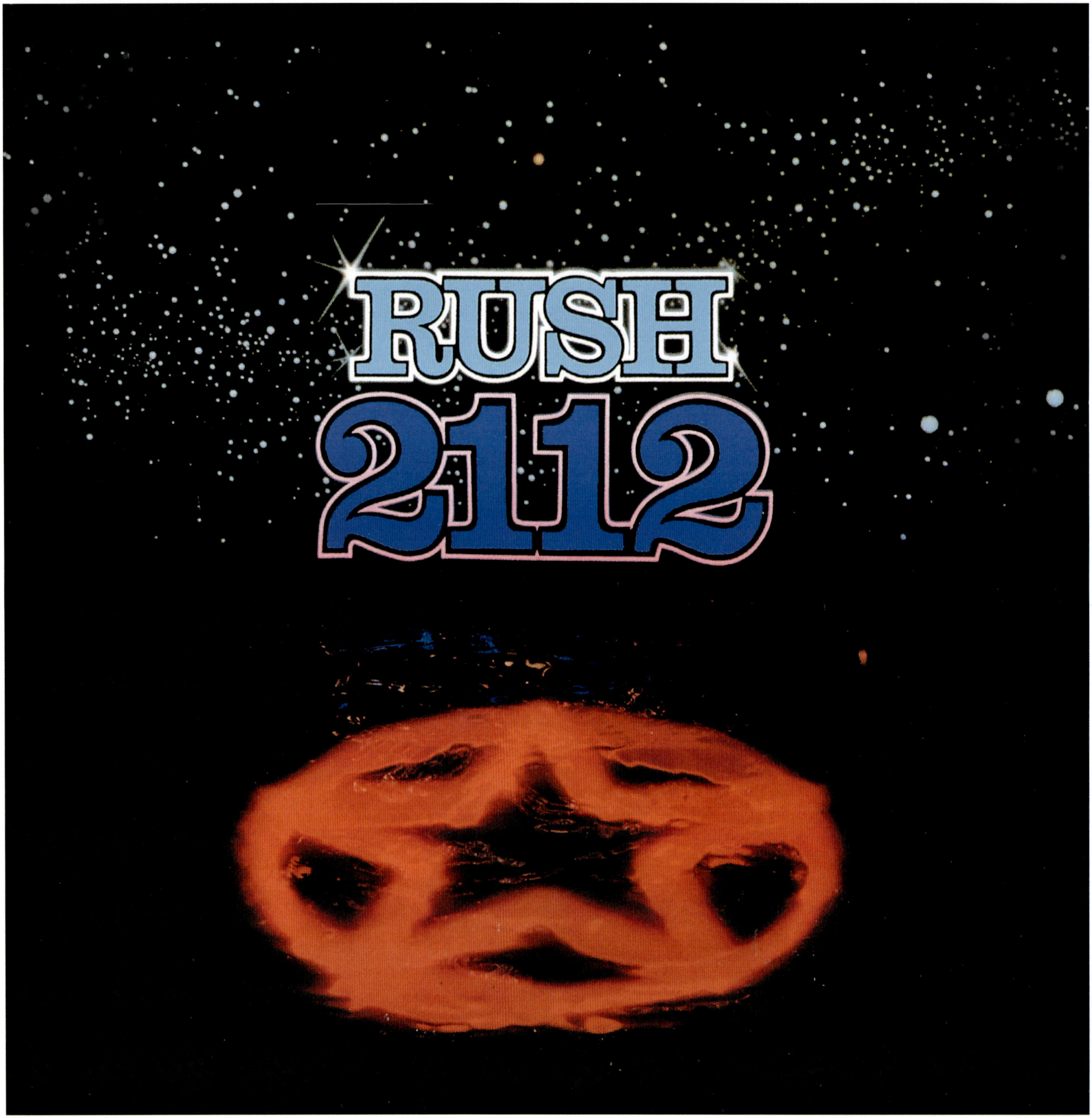
RUSH
2112

AN UNWITTING LOGO

6

LET'S SAY, HYPOTHETICALLY, THAT YOU'RE IN THE BEATLES. You have a bunch of studio records behind you that have turned your band into a cultural phenomenon, so you will also be afforded certain luxuries. For example, you can stop stressing about the cover for your tenth album and put the record into a blank, white jacket, and people will still buy it. Some fans might even collect copies from every pressing of the record since 1968 and put them all over their walls.

Rush, circa 1976, did not have that luxury. They were still looking for their commercial breakthrough, and nothing could be left to chance, particularly the album jacket. It was the first thing consumers would see when they went to the record store, and if it wasn't compelling, it might not doom the record's commercial prospects—but it could certainly create an obstacle at a time when the band really didn't need one.

They had been through that once. Illustrator Hugh Syme had created the album cover for 1975's *Caress of Steel*, his first time at bat for the group. The cover he submitted to Mercury Records underwent a label-directed modification that took Syme's original, sleek, silver design and made it all kinds of brown. If you give neon pink, vibrant magenta, and sun-kissed yellow fingerpaints to a toddler and they smoosh it all together, a mundane, milquetoast brown will result; which was basically what Mercury did to the cover of *Caress of Steel*. Somewhere, Bob Ross is weeping.

When Prometheus Met Gaea

When Peart wrote the story of "2112," he realized partway through that it followed a similar structure to Ayn Rand's 1938 novella *Anthem*. While the Rush epic is its own animal, some thematic points overlap between the suite and the novella. Both are works of dystopian fiction, both take place in the future, and both depict societies in which individuality itself is something the authorities are determined to stamp out. While the suite shares thematic similarities with the novella, the plots are pretty different.

The main character in *Anthem* is a young man whom the state has named Equality 7-2521. He has a sharp mind and is intellectually curious, qualities that are actively discouraged in Rand's novella. In fact, at age 15, every citizen is given a "Life Mandate," otherwise known as the one and only job you're allowed to have for the rest of your life.

This is closely related to something that the government of the Soviet Union used to do, where they would assign you a job for life, and there was nothing you could do about it. Frequently, the job had nothing to do with one's interests, so if you had any personal ambitions, the most you could do was daydream about them on the assembly line at the sausage factory that you were required to work for the next sixty years. Whatever one thinks of Ayn Rand, one can see how it's correct to describe such a situation as oppressive.

While Equality 7-2521 had always dreamed of one day becoming a Scholar and rewarding his intellectual curiosity, the Council of Vocations gives him a Life Mandate of "Street Sweeper." Making any noise about that would only win him additional criminal charges, because in this society, the mere act of wanting to be something other than what your Life Mandate specifies is a crime called "Transgression of Preference."

The story of "2112" and that of *Anthem* continue to diverge, sometimes dramatically. Where the narrator in "2112" transgresses by finding a musical instrument in a cave, Equality 7-2521 sneaks off to a secret laboratory to perform unauthorized science experiments. Also, while the narrator in "2112" is the only flesh-and-blood character in the story, Equality 7-2521 has a love interest, a girl named Liberty 5-3000, whose Life Mandate is "Peasant."

Their star-crossed relationship is also a crime, because Equality 7-2521 and Liberty 5-3000 have willingly chosen each other and freely fallen in love. This stands in contrast to what they're supposed to do, which is get assigned a breeding partner at the "Time of Mating," which sounds like something out of *Midsommar*.

While the narrator's demise in "2112" is a total bummer of a coda, *Anthem* concludes on a note that one could characterize as a Hollywood ending. The couple escapes into the wilderness and pledges to be together forever. Equality 7-2521 changes his name to Prometheus, and Liberty 5-3000 changes hers to Gaea. In the end, they make an Objectivist baby.

Peart could very likely have gotten away with not giving credit to the novella, since the places where they match up mostly have to do with the overall theme. In that sense, "2112" could well owe something to the entire genre of dystopian fiction. George Orwell's *1984* and Aldous Huxley's *Brave New World* depict futures as grim as those in *Anthem* and "2112," and all of the above are stories about the individual against the state, against authority, and against conformity.

At the same time, most who knew Peart described him as ethical and not the type of person who would claim credit for what he perceived as someone else's idea, even if the similarities were inadvertent. Unfortunately, by giving Rand this most basic of professional courtesies, the drummer was associated for life with an ideology that, by his own admission, he had already outgrown in his twenties.

Determined never to let that happen again, Rush instituted a new policy, which guaranteed that the cover Syme submitted would be the cover that went on the record. It even stipulated that he had to be there in person to give his blessing before anyone at the plant threw a switch. This was the right move, because the cover that *2112* received was perfect for it, and it would have been a shame if some kindly but misguided art director from Mercury had decided to "help" the record's sales prospects by mucking everything up again.

The cover that resulted is accepted today as one of the most iconic of all time, but as with so many things that take on that status, it was not planned that way. Syme was a little hazy on some of the details of how the album cover came to be, but give the guy a break—it's been fifty years; and after that kind of expanse of time, it's not unheard of to have some problems remembering why you just went into the kitchen.

"I don't think I am 100% clear how I came up with such a text-driven cover," he said. "But it was certainly through discussions with Neil that we came up with the hero and the oppressive red star of the Solar Federation."

The band used the tried-and-true symbolism of the nude man, which suggested innocence and vulnerability, to depict the hero of the "2112" suite on the cover. He appeared on the LP's inner gatefold, presumably because Sears would not stock your record if it featured a naked man butt hanging out for everyone to see.

"The hero was stripped of all earthly trappings like clothing," Syme said. "He was in his purest form, which is why I asked my friend Bobby to drop trou and let me shoot him from the back. Bobby was in good shape, so I thought he was the perfect candidate."

Syme said that it never once crossed his mind that he was creating an image that would take on a life of its own as the band's logo. Again, sometimes the best things in life are the unplanned ones that fall in your lap.

ABOVE The "unwitting logo" designed by Hugh Syme for *2112* was also used on the cover of the band's first live album, *All the World's a Stage*. The illustrator said he was as surprised as anybody to see it become a permanent fixture in the band's visual imagery.

PREVIOUS Hugh Syme's striking and unmistakable LP cover for *2112*.

SECTOR ONE
SECTOR TWO
SECTOR THREE

On July 19, 2013 *2112* became postage. Thanks to a series of commemorative stamps honoring Canadian recording artists, the "Starman" logo facilitated the end-to-end journey of postcards from Nova Scotia to British Columbia.

"That ended up being an unwitting logo for the band," he said. "It was not our plan that that thing would have such long-lasting impact. It became the band's *Playboy* Bunny, if you will. It's their brand. I really don't know what inspired my approach to the cover, because I've never done a cover like that since. But it's up there with covers like Chicago's, which used just the logo on the cover and has done it as everything from steel to a chocolate bar. I don't quite know why the artwork was all text-driven like that, because it's the only time in my career I really have done that."

In 2016, Geddy Lee co-signed this sentiment in *MOJO*. The group may not have been looking for a logo, and the artist had not necessarily intended to create one. But like a lot of things with this record, it just seemed to fall into place.

"The artwork for the album by our friend Hugh Syme became a brand; it transcended the record and became very representational of us as a band." Geddy Lee to*MOJO* magazine, 2016

In 1982, Peart told *Modern Drummer* what the artwork symbolized and how it related to the album.

"The red star symbolizes the autocratic society that was projected into the future, where giant computers controlled the whole society," he explained. "The star was the symbol of their authority. In a way, it's an abstract symbol for authoritarian governments of any kind, whether they be democratic, dictatorial, or whatever. The man against it, of course, is the individual against this organized state, or anything that's larger than life, whether it be religion, government, or a creed of any kind that's supposed to be more important than a human life."

In 1983, Syme told *CREEM* that the lyrics directly inspired the design. He did not, however, want to be *too* on the nose, so he went for a more symbolic approach. A literal approach, such as depicting some dude in a cave tuning a guitar or standing "atop a spiral stair," may not have worked as well.

"What I did do with that particular cover was read their lyrics, and understand that there is a good force and a bad force," he explained. "The good force was music, creativity, and freedom of expression, and the bad force was anything that was contrary to that. The man is the hero of the story. That he is nude is just a classic tradition . . . the pureness of his person and creativity without the trappings of other elements such as clothing . . . the red star is the evil red star of the Federation."

Another thing Syme said influenced the direction of the cover was his discussions with Peart about the overall theme of the album, the Rand-inspired concept of the individual struggling against the collective. He remem-

"THE ARTWORK FOR THE ALBUM BY OUR FRIEND HUGH SYME BECAME A BRAND; IT TRANSCENDED THE RECORD AND BECAME VERY REPRESENTATIONAL OF US AS A BAND."

GEDDY LEE
to *MOJO* magazine, 2016

bered those decades-old discussions well, and he said they played a significant role in the artistic direction of the album jacket.

"We had long discussions about the Ayn Rand inspiration," he said. "This was a hero pushing against oppressive, anti-freedom, anti-creative forces."

In addition to featuring the "Starman" character, the gatefold sleeve also afforded pothead Rush fans the ideal surface to clean all the seeds and stems out of the eighth they had just bought. All the lyrics were printed on the inner gatefold, so you could even perform this task right on top of the lyrics to the cannabis travelogue, "A Passage to Bangkok."

The back cover featured the track listing and the journaling of the song's narrator. He refers to "Twin Moons" and watching "Templevision" and, of course, "the Red Star of the Solar Federation." The text is credited to "Anonymous, 2112."

People looking at the album for the first time without ever hearing it must have wondered what all that referred to exactly, and it's possible that a few record shoppers read it, found it too impenetrable, and bought Anne Murray's *Keeping in Touch* instead. It's also entirely possible that nobody even bothered to read any of that text because they were too busy taking in the sight of the Rush members posing in kimonos, an act that they will never live down and which they have wisely chosen to laugh about, along with the rest of us.

7

2112 FOR DUMMIES

SO WHAT THE HELL WAS THE "2112" STORY ABOUT ANYWAY? For those who never got to have Neil Peart explain it to us in person, it might be a little challenging to glean from the lyric sheet alone. You might guess it takes place in the future and is about an individual in an oppressive society, but the lyrics don't spell everything out explicitly. What was a fan who wanted a deeper understanding of the story to do?

If those fans went to see Rush on their *2112* tour, they were given a tour program containing an attempt by the band to explain the story. It was still pretty inscrutable, but it was nice of the band to try to unpack it.

One of the venues at which the tour program was distributed was Toronto's Massey Hall. The band performed there on three consecutive nights in June 1976, and those concerts were recorded for the group's first live album, *All the World's a Stage*. Those who opened the program on one of those nights found a page with the header "The Story of '2112,'" which laid out the story of the suite in four concise paragraphs. Each plot point in the prose corresponds to a movement from the full "2112" suite, as in "a man discovers what was once known years before as a guitar ('Discovery')."

The story takes place in the titular year, half a century after a 2062 galactic war that ends with all the planets falling under the iron-fisted rule of the Solar Federation. Its reign over the galaxy is Draconian and brutal, and it exercises control over the population with computers called "Temples."

The Temples function like the Ministry of Truth in George Orwell's *1984*, and they have already gone to the trouble of creating a state-approved slate of acceptable books, albums, and television shows. The tragic part is that half a century after this

Lifeson, Lee, and Peart at London's Hammersmith Odeon on February 20, 1978. They're joined onstage by the modest keyboard setup that would become Geddy's gateway drug with synthesizers.

PREVIOUS Lifeson performs some fretboard acrobatics while Peart and Lee use the opportunity to execute some unimaginably complex rhythmic feats in unison.

HIWATT
HIWATT
HIWATT

cautionary suite was written, consumers might be totally fine with having all their entertainment chosen in advance by the government and might even pay a $16.99 monthly subscription fee for the privilege.

The narrator, symbolized by the naked figure in the gatefold, is a denizen of this soul-crushing dictatorship. He finds a guitar in a cave and enthusiastically reports back to the Temples to tell the priests of his discovery, but they're not having any of it, and they tell him, "It doesn't fit the plan."

The narrator returns to the cave, where he dreams of an oracle, who leads him to a place of peace and beauty. It's a vision of life from before the galactic war and before the current tyranny. Like every dream we don't want to wake up from, it feels completely real, making it all the more jarring and traumatic when he wakes up to find he's still a resident of the Solar Federation. At that point, he takes his own life, which almost seems like a rational act in the face of an existence in that society.

As he dies, another galactic war begins. Maybe if he had been more of a laggard and not set about dying by suicide so expeditiously, he could have lived in a post–Solar Federation galaxy. We never find out, though. The story ends there, unresolved and open to interpretation.

BELOW Lifeson and Lee back-to-back on stage in one of their frequent moments of good-natured goofiness.

LEFT Neil Peart strikes a pose, shrouded in eerie fog.

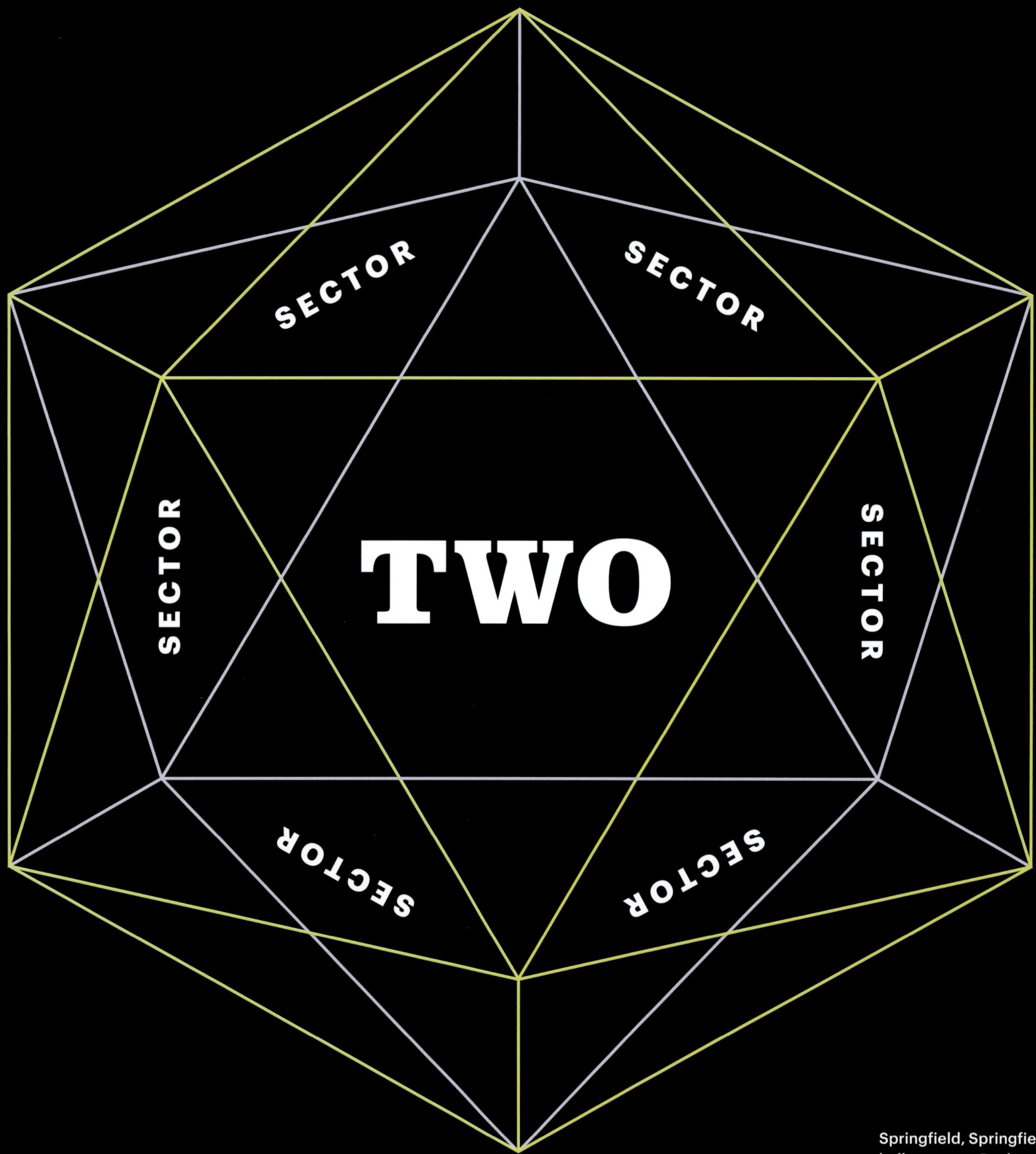

Springfield, Springfield, it's a helluva town. Rush at the Civic Center in Springfield, Massachusetts, on December 9, 1976.

RUSH
neil
RUSH
peart

SIDE ONE

1

I. 2112

Music by Geddy Lee & Alex Lifeson, lyrics by Neil Peart,
"With acknowledgement to the genius of Ayn Rand"

The "2112" suite takes up all of the album's side one, clocking in at 20:33. It's the longest song Rush ever recorded, exceeding "The Fountain of Lamneth" from side two of *Caress of Steel*, whose running time is 20:06. While no one at Mercury Records ever said to them, "We want you to stop putting 20:06 suites on the second side of your records," it is wryly amusing to imagine the band receiving this instruction and then doing exactly what they asked—after all, "2112" is neither on side two, nor is it 20:06 in length.

Putting the band's longest epic first on the record may well have been intended to be a poke in the eye to those who wished to constrain their artistic vision. Still, it's much more likely that it received that placement because the band was proud of it, and it was unquestionably the album's centerpiece. So, why should they put that last? Also, if the worst came to pass and *2112* sold not one copy but came out the way the band wanted, that was cool by them. Like any self-respecting *Project Runway* designer, they were willing to say *auf Wiedersehen* over draping they believed in.

Analyzing the suite movement by movement may seem like a redundant exercise. By now, everyone has heard it, everyone knows how the song goes, and everyone knows the fate of the poor narrator. The suite has been listened to on every format in every decade since the 1970s. While kids today don't listen to it on eight-track in an airbrushed cruising van filled with pot smoke, they're listening to it on Spotify through AirPods, presumably while vaping.

What follows is a rundown of all the music on side one of *2112*, which amounts to a single extended track. The suite was clearly inspired by the Who's *Tommy*, but instead of stretching it out to seventy-five minutes with lots of filler and twelve-second songs, Rush showed restraint and capped it at one album side. It's not all that hard to imagine adolescent Geddy and Alex listening to *Tommy* in the Weinrib family basement and coming up for air from the bowels of side three to ask, "Could this be shorter and still tell the same story?"

Overture

"2112" features exactly two nods to classical music, both of which occur in this first movement. The first comes in the form of a brief snippet of Pyotr Ilyich Tchaikovsky's "The Year 1812, Solemn Overture, Op. 49." This piece of music is better known as "The 1812 Overture," and Rush's miniature tribute to it even has the sound of firing cannons, just like the original. Apart from that, the only other nod to classical music comes from the fact that they call the first movement an overture.

Still, Dr. R. Douglas Helvering, composer and host of the *Daily Doug* YouTube channel, said that we can consider this a genuine overture, because those aren't limited only to classical music. Just ask any theater geek.

"The idea of an overture containing a bunch of the themes that you'll hear—specifically and right on the nose so that nobody can miss them—comes from the old classic Broadway musicals," he said. "*Oklahoma*, *My Fair Lady*, *Carousel*, *West Side Story*, *South Pacific*, those types of things."

He said that one would also frequently encounter an overture at the beginning of the great epic movies of classic Hollywood, even those that weren't musicals. Both the 1962 David Lean epic *Lawrence of Arabia* and Stanley Kubrick's 1968 science fiction masterpiece *2001: A Space Odyssey* opened with overtures, both of which set the

RIGHT It's May 13, 1979, at Southampton's Gaumont in England, and Geddy Lee appears to give his highest rating to standing next to a wardrobe with the door ajar. Neil Peart is reading a book, per custom.

PREVIOUS Rush in Bakersfield, California, on September 26, 1977.

RUSTLER
Give it a Shot
On!

BELOW Alex Lifeson and Geddy Lee backstage on December 9, 1976. Lee scowls as though admonished by Mary Weinrib to keep it down in the basement, you two.

RIGHT The *2112 Days* bootleg, which documents the band's October 28, 1976, performance in Seattle after a month-long tour of their native Canada.

ABOVE Alex Lifeson is all smiles at Le Studio in Morin Heights, Quebec, during the October 1979 *Permanent Waves* sessions, the first of the final three studio records co-produced by Terry Brown.

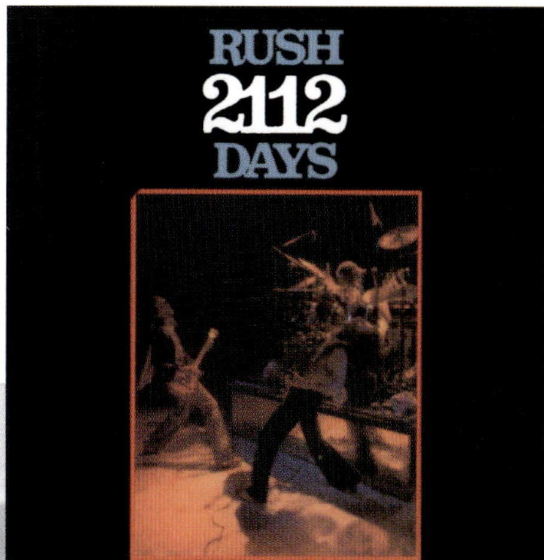

scene for what people were about to watch. It also allowed them to get settled in for the ride ahead, dialing up the audience's investment in the scene, the characters, and the story.

"You remember watching the old movies, and it was like, 'Why am I watching eight minutes of credits first before I watch anything else?'" Dr. Helvering said. "That's the overture, and it comes from the Broadway show. It's a way to showcase the tunes that they're going to hear. Broadway musicals started out as a vehicle for popular songs. . . . 'Overture' is the longest section of the suite, which can often happen if you're going to include a bunch of stuff."

The word derives from the French *ouverture* and translates to "opening." It dates back to the seventeenth century. Even in the late eighteenth century, composers of the Romantic era like Beethoven found that you didn't even necessarily need to have an entire opera or oratorio to justify having an overture. These composers just went ahead and composed their own freestanding overtures, utterly independent of any larger work.

The movement begins with science fiction sounds reminiscent of the original *Star Trek*, with lots of whooshing and swooshing noises to suggest traveling through a mysterious cosmos into an undiscovered celestial body. After those forty-six seconds, it becomes a "proper" overture in that it sends out miniature teaser versions of most of the motifs you'll hear in roman numerals ii–vii.

The band play all of it with a ferocity that one doesn't hear often from them. You can tell from the energetic rage in the performance that this is personal to them, this means something to them, and they were betting all their chips on it.

There are other highlights and details. In the middle breakdown section of the overture, Lifeson plays a dramatic, pained guitar solo that immediately takes its place as one of the best he ever recorded in the studio. Leading up to it, there's a section during which Lee sings some ascending vocals mixed to fit into the surroundings without sounding like a human voice. It wasn't until people bought *All the World's a Stage* or saw the band perform live that they realized it was Geddy, son of Morris, doing the honors.

The most addictive part comes toward its end, during a few bouncy bars of minor-key guitar chords that are a little reminiscent of "Fire on High" by Electric Light Orchestra. When the song was performed live, audiences would respond to the pauses in that section by chanting "hey" between each one, an activity normally more popular at sporting events than musical ones.

Of all seven movements in the "2112" suite, "Overture" was written last. Lifeson unpacked it in the liner notes to the *2112* 40th Anniversary Edition.

"When we started putting 'Overture' together, we knew what the sequence was, it was just a matter of going through those main themes . . . and changing the arrangements in such a way that they connected to each other better, rather than having a sense that they were a little more standalone," he said. "In 'Overture' the connection is a lot tighter, you get everything across as quickly as possible, you make slight adjustments in some of the riffs and themes to make the pacing a little quicker and more connected. . . . I think 'Overture' for '2112' is really a solid representation of the whole record. It distills it to this really cool opening."

The opening whooshing and swooshing noises were provided by cover illustrator Hugh Syme, who performed them on an ARP Odyssey synthesizer. He had not come to the studio intending to play music. He just happened to be there.

"I was in the studio at the right time," he said. "Knowing them as well as I did—I was in a band on the same label—they already knew that I played keys. They liked how I played, apparently. Geddy and I, as friends, would get together at my place, and I would just be noodling and playing stuff, and he would casually say, 'What was that?' I'd say, 'Oh, it's just messing around.' He would look at me and say, 'I hate you.' As keyboard players go, he was very creative and very inventive and very sonically astute in what he accomplished, but he was never a piano player, like Tony Banks or even myself. I took piano for eight years, so it's just sort of in my genes."

He appeared on the "2112" overture at the invitation of co-producer Terry Brown. After all, Syme was there, so why not?

"I was kind of surprised when Terry said, 'Here, come out with something for the overture, something really spicy,'" Syme recalled. "I had my ARP Odyssey synthesizer there, and I was pretty familiar with all of its envelopes and its tone generator, so I just sat on the floor, and Geddy held down a bass note on the synthesizer. We were both kind of lying on the floor. We did about three passes, but I created the envelope effects, the texture, and the kind of sweeping sounds."

Brown recalled that during the recording, the band made great use of an Eventide digital delay that he had rented for Toronto Sound, which was doing well but still had some budgetary limitations.

"It was a small studio," he said. "We were young and didn't have a whole lot of finances, so I rented an Eventide digital delay. I remember we were sitting, playing with it, and you could throw

Kneel before Ged. Lifeson, Lee, and Peart at the International Amphitheater in Chicago on December 14, 1978.

Alex Lifeson plays what looks like an open G chord through Marshall stacks on the *All the World's a Stage* tour.

a switch, and you could put voices or instruments up the octave or down the octave. I remember us sitting there playing with that and laughing hysterically over it. because it was so much fun. We used it a lot on that record, in a more substantial way, I might add."

"Overture" concludes with an up-tempo section that sees Alex throw in a theme from Tchaikovsky's "1812 Overture," followed by an explosion (or is it more cannon fire?). After the smoke and debris clear, Alex picks some nylon-string guitar, allowing Lee to quote the Bible, a rare occurrence in a band whose primary lyric writer didn't believe in god.

"And the meek shall inherit the earth." After that, it's off to the races, and the suite begins in earnest.

While it's understandable if some view the previous four-plus minutes as a self-indulgent exercise, Dr. Helvering insisted that it's appropriate for the song and the band, who were trying to paint on a larger canvas than they had ever done before. Besides, don't we all sometimes do our own overtures if we have something important to lay on people?

"An overture is kind of an ancient part of human rhetoric," he said. "When we give a speech, we start with an introduction, and you tell them what you're going to say. We have ways of repeating ideas that make sense to the human brain as you're experiencing it, without the help of being able to record it and rewatch it and re-experience it. We have prologues in literature and for music, especially with multi-movement pieces or multi-sectional, substantial pieces."

II. The Temples of Syrinx

If anyone was unclear that Rush had a lot on their minds as they recorded *2112*, that notion comes across in the music of "Overture." If that still wasn't enough, the second movement, "The Temples of Syrinx," explicitly spells it out for them. The aforementioned rage in the vocals and lyrics and a light patina of anxiety suggest the song takes place during some "interesting times," as the axiom goes. Dr. Helvering said it's

“WHAT IS THE ROLE OF THE ARTIST IN THE CULTURE? WHAT IS THE ROLE OF THE PERSON WHO IS CREATIVE, THE PERSON WHO IS THE NON-CONFORMIST, THE PERSON WHO GOES AGAINST THE CROWD?”

DONNA HALPER to author, 2025

Anarchy in the T.O.

In 1976, several albums were released that formed the foundation for punk rock. The self-titled Ramones album was one of them, featuring fourteen songs clocking in at twenty-nine minutes, including "Blitzkrieg Bop," "Beat on the Brat," and "Now I Wanna Sniff Some Glue." The self-titled Blondie album was also released, featuring such classics as "X Offender" and "Rip Her to Shreds." And let's not forget Richard Hell and the Voidoids, whose *Another World* EP featured the early punk anthem "Blank Generation."

Those are all fine and good, but the best punk rock album released in 1976 was *2112*. All those other releases came from people who were just pretending.

You see, when punk rock bands walked onstage for the first time, they had nothing to lose. Rush, meanwhile, potentially had their entire career to lose. They saved it by staying true to their vision and refusing to compromise, which is pretty punk rock.

Musically, there is not a single note of punk to be found anywhere on *2112*. That musical style is based on short songs, disqualifying the Canadian trio from the outset. Also, Lifeson's guitars are tuned, and Peart lands his fills in time. While no punk rock music resides within the grooves of *2112*, the attitude is there in spades.

This proposition deserves some unpacking. If we understand the punk rock attitude to be, "We all have mohawks, we gob at the band performing onstage, and we're all on the dole," then, no, there is no punk rock attitude to be found on *2112*. On the other hand, if we define "punk" as a defiant stance against authority and a determination to express oneself honestly, then Rush was punk AF, and *2112* was their two-fingered salute to those who sought to fence them in.

Lee acknowledged that, just prior to *2112*, the band's eyes may have been bigger than their stomach. Their reach may have exceeded their grasp. After all, on the album preceding *2112*, the last two songs took up thirty-three of the album's forty-five minutes. They had pulled an Icarus and flown too close to the sun, and now they plummeted earthward, their artistic hubris leaving a cloud of wax-encrusted feathers in their wake.

"Nobody really understood what the hell we were doing with that record," the bassist said in the liner notes for the *2112* 40th Anniversary Edition. Indeed, Lifeson said that the response was not positive when he played the record for Paul Stanley from KISS. To his credit, the Star Child nodded politely as the music played, so at least he wasn't a douche about it. He was a bellwether, however. The public was lukewarm, the tour was a bust, and the record didn't sell.

Many musicians would have thrown in the towel right then and there. Many record labels would have, too. Luckily, Mercury Records didn't exercise their option to drop the band.

Despite fearing that *2112* might usher in the end of Rush's career, the label was pleasantly surprised to see it start selling. Suddenly, the exact thing they had said they didn't want—a sprawling prog epic with no single—was now just what the doctor ordered.

Peart said its success was all the sweeter because it directly rebuked the label, which thought it knew best. When Mercury's fears were allayed, it effectively killed the idea that Rush needed to be more commercial. From that point forward, the label took a hands-off approach to the band, which came in handy as they experimented with different styles on subsequent albums. They had won their freedom and done it the punk rock way.

If you are still skeptical of Rush's punk rock bona fides, look no further than season one, episode three of the British television comedy *The Young Ones*. The show aired from 1982 to 1984 on BBC2 and featured the exploits of four young male roommates. Each represented a

Vyvyan Basterd (Ade Edmondson) wears a t-shirt depicting his favorite punk rock album in this "Sick" episode.

particular youth subculture, so there was a hippie, a freewheeling ladies' man, and a grating cosplay anarchist whom viewers wanted to punch in the face.

In addition to those three was the punk character, Vyvyan Basterd, who wore a Rush T-shirt in the "Sick" episode, which aired on June 12, 1984. It appeared to be some off-brand, unofficial *2112* shirt; but he wore it nonetheless. Case closed.

In 2023, Lee told readers of the *Guardian* that he had loving memories of the punk era, if not punk music. He didn't spin any Exploited records at home, but his warm feelings remained.

"I remember it quite fondly, because we were mixing an album in London when the Sex Pistols were on TV," he said. "It was fascinating to watch. At the same time, the three-chord style of these bands instantly made us seem like Beethoven by comparison."

as effective as it is because "Overture" did its job and fully primed the pump for it.

"There are some musical nods to the rest of the piece that I hear in 'Overture,'" he said. "Primarily, I think it's just nodding to the next section, to 'The Temples of Syrinx,' and that opening guitar—bum, bum!—comes back at the beginning of 'The Temples of Syrinx' a little bit."

He explained how some motifs that made a brief appearance in "Overture" get a more fully developed treatment in "The Temples of Syrinx." At first, we only got a teaser.

"In that next song, we get the same key," he said. "When they say, 'We are the priests,' that moves up to B minor, and it's the same music that they had been doing in 'Overture' with the same progressions. They were just applying it with a little bit of a different drum pattern and then overlaying the lyrics there."

That section is sung by the priests, who cannot say enough good things about the totalitarian police state they've installed. Creative expression may get you thrown in prison, but why should you "need to wonder how or why" when they've already made all your decisions for you?

If Mercury Records wanted a single off *2112*, a standalone 45 rpm featuring just "The Temples of Syrinx" might have done the job nicely. Indeed, most Rush compilation albums that seek to anthologize the band's studio output will merge "Overture" with this movement and include nothing further past that point. After all, you can't put a 20:33 song on a single-disc "greatest hits" compilation.

The movement comes charging out of the gate at full volume from the entire band and contains one of Lee's most aggressive vocal deliveries. In a couple of bits, it's almost piercing enough to be classified as a weapon. It's kind of amazing that he can do that while being his typical virtuoso bassist self, sending his fingers up and down the fretboard in ways no other bassist would consider.

The whole thing is only a little over two minutes long, but after "Overture" has stated all the musical

Geddy Lee goes full kimono on his Rickenbacker 4080 double-neck guitar on the *All the World's a Stage* tour.

motifs, it's the perfect introduction to the actual plot and sets the scene perfectly. The priests even start by saying they've "taken care of everything," making a miserable life under the boot of oppression sound like an all-expenses-paid cruise to the Bahamas with unlimited free drinks.

III. Discovery

To the extent that the "2112" suite drags at all, it tends to do so in the spots that are more about the plot than the music. On a songwriting level, this section is totally unnecessary and doesn't move the music along very much. It's crucial to the plot, however, so in it goes.

The movement depicts the narrator, who finds a "strange device" in a cave. It's a long-forgotten guitar, a relic of the time before the interplanetary war. Donna Halper said that even though the drummer wrote the lyrics, it had to be a guitar that the narrator finds, due to its long history as the instrument of choice for anyone wishing to stick it to the man.

"The topics that he was interested in are still very relevant to today," she said. "What is the role of the artist in the culture? What is the role of the person who is creative, the person who is the non-conformist, the person who goes against the crowd? It's no accident that on Woody Guthrie's guitar, it had a little sign on it that said, 'This machine kills fascists.'"

Indeed, it wouldn't have worked for the narrator to find a drum kit, as it has severe limitations when it comes to creating folkie protest songs. "Blowin' in the Wind" would simply not be the same song with Bob Dylan accompanying himself on a crash cymbal.

"This was so important to Neil," she said. "It wasn't going to be drums. It was going to be something that could make lyrics, something that could speak truth to power, something that could stand up and be thought-provoking. That's not what society wanted. That's not what the culture wanted. In a way, it was almost kind of like a middle finger to the record label. It was like, 'You want us to conform, you want us to be like everyone else. You want us to do this and that, and we are not doing it.'"

While much has been said about Rush as a progressive rock band, Dr. Helvering was not sure the label applies. Sure, "2112" is over twenty minutes long, certainly making it prog-adjacent. But musically, he said there's not much happening that you would hear on an Emerson, Lake & Palmer record. He said it's much closer to heavy metal and hard rock stylistically, but given a progressive spin.

"This is real rock and roll, not necessarily progressive rock like the Canterbury scene or anything like that," he said. "I hear more Rush in heavy metal and heavy rock bands than I do in progressive or almost jazz fusion bands. I think they're closer to that realm than the other. So it makes sense to me that a band like Metallica appreciates the storytelling and the production, and the balls of these guys, just to put out what they want."

While the "Discovery" movement of "2112" is no *Lulu*, Rush caught a lot of flak regardless for doing things of that nature. They were regularly described as self-indulgent in the press, and again, two minutes of a guitar being tuned against the backdrop of water sounds may seem to some critics like a selfish waste of vinyl. But if you're doing prog rock, even prog rock that doesn't sound like prog rock, you get to do what you want.

Dr. Helvering pointed out that, unlike the other movements, nothing from "Discovery" appears in "Overture." He also pointed out that it gives the listener's ears a break after the heaviness of "The Temples of Syrinx."

"The music completely changes with Alex in the 'Discovery' section, with the acoustic guitar," he said. "There's nothing of foreshadowing of that in 'Overture,' and rightfully so. It would ruin the surprise."

According to the liner notes in the *2112* 40th anniversary box set, the water noises came from a sound effects record, a relic of the twentieth century. In 1976, you could walk into a record store and buy a piece of vinyl consisting of nothing but the sound of barking dogs, doors slamming, and glass shattering. We owe the sonic collage that is "Discovery" to this bygone artifact.

Once "Discovery" becomes more of an actual song, Geddy sings in a softer and more subdued style than on the more hard-rocking movements. Lifeson said it was one of the last things written for the suite and happened without any toil. His part was recorded in one shot, with no overdubs, as he imagined himself in the cave the narrator finds.

"It was kind of a stream of consciousness arrangement, sitting in the control room in Toronto Sound with everybody around," he said.

If "Discovery" sounds familiar to you, please consult side one of the Who's *Tommy* and play "Amazing Journey," which Lifeson said the band used to play during their bar band days.

"In our earliest days, we played the version of 'Amazing Journey' that was on *Live at Leeds*," he said. "Definitely on an acoustic guitar I tend to lean towards Pete Townshend and the kind of chords he plays and the way he plays. He plays in some chordal positions that a lot of other people don't. He's great at that sort of thing, taking traditional block chording and then moving it up around the neck."

"Discovery" is 100% exposition and barely functions as a song. Still, it's crucial to the story, since we wouldn't have one if the narrator didn't find a guitar in a cave in the first place. At the same time, the section was deemed so surplus to requirements that when the band performed the whole suite live, they would usually skip roman numeral iii entirely.

Lifeson's chordal tribute to Pete Townshend effectively provides a lighter texture and brief interlude before the next section, which sees the band back at full volume. The section did get a live airing on 1998's *Different Stages*, and it saw Lifeson do some interesting modal solo playing with a pastoral, folky feel. It wouldn't be out of place alongside Led Zeppelin's "Black Mountain Side." It's a very neat bit of playing from Lifeson, and it extends what they were going for in this section, making it more exotic.

IV. Presentation

"Presentation" is a good example of Rush learning from "The Fountain of Lamneth" and developing each movement into more of a "proper" song. At no time does the listener think, "Oh my god, not this riff again," as they might have done during side two of *Caress of Steel*. Furthermore, there are neither didacts nor narpets anywhere to be found.

"It's both raw and polished at the same time because they allow so much room for the fuzz on Geddy's bass and the fact that they don't have anybody really playing rhythm," Dr. Helvering said. "A lot of the music just has this visceral nature."

"Presentation" could be a song in its own right. It starts very heavy and switches back and forth between quieter textures when the narrator is talking, then crushingly heavy ones when the priests are talking. It is also worth mentioning that Peart uses this opportunity to execute all kinds of superhuman rolls and fills and cymbal

Lifeson plays his Gibson EDS-1275 and Lee plays his Rickenbacker 4080, while Peart leverages state-of-the-art 1976 riser technology for his kit.

Marshall
Marshall

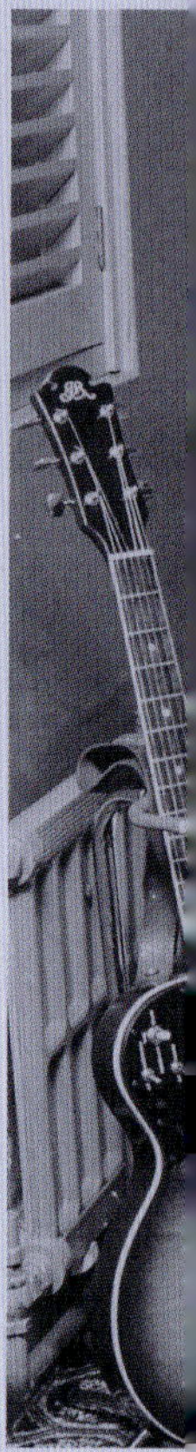

ABOVE "I could play anything. That was the real benefit." Lifeson credited his 1972 classical guitar lessons with broadening his technique and keeping his chops up.

LEFT Ready or not, here we come. *RPM Weekly* devotes valuable ink and real estate to a band hoping their fourth album sells better than their third.

FAR LEFT Geddy Lee leans into it at the Civic Center in Springfield, Massachusetts, December 9, 1976.

crashes during those bits, especially when the priests came back the second time around. At that point, he embarks on an extended journey across the toms just after the line, "We have our work to do," and it seems to justify at least 65 percent of his forty-piece drum kit of later years.

Everything then goes into double time while Lifeson solos like crazy. One might presume that it symbolizes the bouncer outside the priests' velvet ropes ejecting our narrator from the Temples of Syrinx.

Also worth mentioning is that this is the song in which Lee proves he could have been cast in multiple roles in a production of *Jesus Christ Superstar*. He takes the roles of both the narrator and the priests, and when he sings as the narrator, his approach is gentle and almost humble, as if to show deference. To return the favor, the Geddy-priests shriek at him in his highest possible register and reject him for wasting their time with some relic from an ancient culture. He could have played at least two of the Pharisees with no problem.

V. Oracle: The Dream

Not to keep harping on the unfortunate and misunderstood "The Fountain of Lamneth," but the "2112" suite suggests that they had grown past whatever limitations held that composition back from being fully realized. The use of dynamics is leaps and bounds ahead of it, and the level of emotion is much more palpable. They're not just playing riffs and doing neat drum fills—there's purpose and determination here.

"Oracle: The Dream" functions as a callback to "Discovery" in the sense that it's a more subdued piece whose lighter texture is meant to act as an interlude from the heavier stuff. It starts with solo guitar and a subdued Geddy vocal, then goes into a heavier, full-band section at mid-tempo. Also, like "Discovery," it's less of a song in its own right and more of a two-minute exercise that moves the story along.

There's nothing wrong with it, and the performance is at the same elite level as everything else

Alex Lifeson bends the E string until it cries for absolution during the 1976 *All the World's a Stage* tour.

EVENTIDE DIGITAL DELAY
LAST BAG

The interior of the McMorran Arena in Port Huron, Michigan, just hours before the show on May 22, 1977, and eons prior to the upcoming interplanetary war.

on the record. Having said that, if you were to take the *Different Stages* version of "2112," which is kindly indexed into separate tracks for each movement, you may conclude that it's more of an expository endeavor than an actual "verse- chorus- verse- chorus-'I love you' bridge-verse-chorus-end" song. Not that there's anything wrong with that.

"It's more narrative," Dr. Helvering said. "It's part of this really engrossing story, rather than relying on formal divisions to help give it context."

He added that it also helps that we already heard it in teaser form during "Overture."

"Having an overture that's thematic is a lot more important, because all we have are the melodies and the phrases and the cadences of the music itself to tie back to it," he said. "With the lyrics, we can follow the story even if the music doesn't have any sort of formal division. We understand what's going on in the story, and the music reflects what's happening in the present time. That's why it doesn't necessarily need to rely on any sort of formal devices that Strauss would have used as he was writing his tone poems."

VI. Soliloquy

According to the *2112* 40th anniversary box set, "Soliloquy" was originally called "Soliloquy of the Soul. " It opens with another lonely, open acoustic motif that recalls the introduction to "More Than a Feeling" before the mighty Sib Hashian starts pounding the skins. It's accompanied by a gentle Lee vocal and features the last lyrics of the entire suite.

The movement finds our narrator in pretty rough shape. He's back at the cave where he found the guitar, and after his dream, in which the oracle shows him how life used to be before the galaxy-wide war, he succumbs to utter hopelessness. In the year 2112, there is no teletherapy or dialectical behavioral principles. There isn't even any of *Brave New World*'s "soma" to take the edge off. Lacking any such therapeutic options, he takes his own life.

Lee turns in an emotional vocal performance here, and one notices that he's becoming a more confident singer, an artisan at the microphone, and not just the band's singer because no one else wanted to do it. The critics, of course, didn't see it that way; but by this point, the band surely knew they would never get a fair shake from them.

In the second half, the whole band comes in at a slow and lumbering tempo, making it one of the group's heaviest moments. Lee's vocal goes back to anguished shrieking, and it sounds like the whole band is collectively despairing right along with him as he sings that he doesn't know if he can carry on.

Again with the shrieking, this guy. One wonders if, in addition to crafting hit singles, it wasn't also hoped at the label that Lee might dial it back a bit, too, so maybe they could get a nice review from Robert Christgau. Well, that's an emphatic "no." The band stayed true to their vision, and if anyone had any problems with any of it, they were free to stop complaining, go home, and listen to James Taylor. Take it or leave it. Dr. Helvering said Rush was a perfect case of a band that you could only ruin by removing what the haters would have called "the flaws."

"I've often thought, 'What if Rush were founded as a four-piece, with an extra singer that played rhythm guitar, and it was a different voice,'" he said. "Geddy could just play keyboards and bass and maybe do backing vocals. But would we like them as much? Would it come off the same? Would the vocals be in the same register? Would it have the same point of view?"

He concluded that Rush minus the attributes that earned them so much critical hatred was unlikely to work. You could smooth those things out, but you would lose everything that made

“IT’S ROCK AND ROLL, IT’S SCI-FI, IT’S BEAUTIFUL, IT’S HARSH, IT’S ELECTRONIC, IT’S ACOUSTIC,” HE SAID. “IT’S PRETTY SPECTACULAR. IT REALLY IS. IT’S KIND OF A UNICORN.”

DR. HELVERING
to author, 2025

This LP pressing of Rush’s much-bootlegged December 5, 1974, show is adorned by a 1978 photo of the band and Terry Brown, presumably to annoy chronology-conscious Rush fans.

them the band that they were, and that won a hardcore fan base by never compromising one iota.

He added that it wasn't just a case of the vocal. This band was utterly unique in everything they did, so even if they found a less polarizing singer, there were still all those drum solos and twenty-minute songs about authoritarianism to deal with. They were who they were, and there was no "fixing" it. Everything about the band was perfectly balanced, and just one "improvement" could destroy the whole thing. Love them or hate them, Lee's vocals perfectly fit what the band set out to accomplish.

VII. Grand Finale

As befits a twenty-minute suite about a future dystopia, "2112" does not have a happy ending. Since the "Grand Finale" movement has no lyrics, we have no idea what to make of the ending. The band doesn't specify it, allowing every listener to choose their own adventure. Having said that, the end of the movement, suite, and album side sounds very much like it's the end of the world.

The movement opens with another riff that sounds like an outtake from *Who's Next* and features a straight-ahead rock rhythm that they ride for a little bit. That comes to a dead stop and shifts into an insistent, unexpected riff in 6/8 time. The band then goes off with much cymbal crashing, metallic guitar, and Lee going right ahead and murdering his Rickenbacker fretboard. The band concludes the festivities with a big meltdown and an ominous announcement that could mean a lot of things.

"In the end, our protagonist is crushed," Halper said. "'Attention all planets of the Solar Federation, we have assumed control.' But as long as there's music, as long as there's art, as long as there's creativity, we're not done yet, even though this is a dystopian fantasy. There are still things to say."

She added that even if the worst interpretation of the ending is true, creative types are still more likely to be inspired than demoralized by "2112." Maybe the narrator is gone, but other nonconformists, insurgents, and dissenters will take his place. In this way, the suite functions both as a cautionary tale and as a call to action. If you're a creative person and you don't like the world around you, stand up and be heard. Do something about it.

"Inherent in being an artist is wanting to make people think about your art," she said. "The artist doesn't want to be the one whose spirit is crushed. So '2112' is both a fantasy and a warning."

Lifeson said in the *2112* 40th anniversary box set that even though a lot of people call the suite a concept piece, he considers it more of an opera.

"You are sitting out in the audience and watching scene changes," he said of how the suite plays out for him. "It feels like chapters that you're reading, and it is very visual. Everything has its character and when it is repeated it reminds you of what that is."

"It's rock and roll, it's sci-fi, it's beautiful, it's harsh, it's electronic, it's acoustic," he said. "It's pretty spectacular. It really is. It's kind of a unicorn."

Dr. Helvering didn't use the term "opera"—or worse yet, "rock opera"—to describe "2112." He said that if he had to give it some kind of label, it would have to be "a science fiction rock and roll suite."

"I mean, they do name the different sections," he said. "They're definitely segmented and very clear to follow."

Finally, he said that it isn't surprising to him that people have continued to respond to this album for decades, and he expects that trend to continue. He said it occupies a unique niche in music history, and that's likely to keep people curious and engaged for a long time to come. It comes down to one thing, something you can't buy at a music store and can never learn—originality.

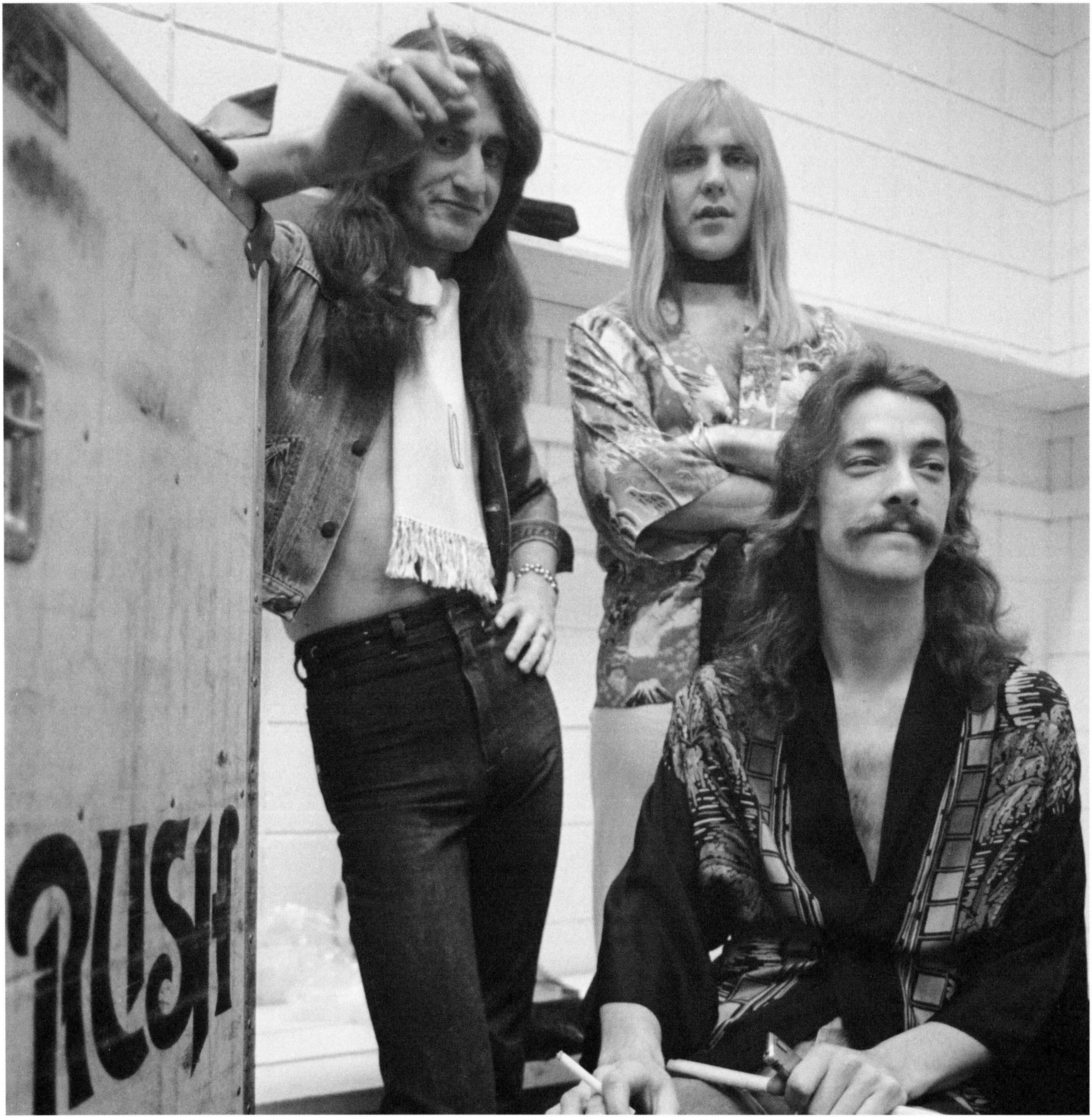
RUSH

SIDE TWO

2112 IS FREQUENTLY CALLED A CONCEPT ALBUM, but that's not accurate in the strictest sense of the term. None of the five songs on its second side are related to the story on the first, so half the record's duration has nothing to do with Megadon, the Red Star, or the year 2112. It's based on the Planet Earth of the here and now.

Still, despite the change of setting and subject matter, you can't say this half of the record is unrelated to the first. Its two sides together comprise a unified piece of work that gets a theme across to listeners, if not a plot.

There was already a precedent for this. Country singer Johnny Cash was making records considered concept pieces since 1960's *Ride This Train*. That album consists of eight songs that have nothing to do with each other but for the fact that they're about trains. By that standard, *2112* is a concept album, and side two is part of that.

"Something for Nothing" neatly restates the "2112" theme of individual expression in an efficient and compact form. Songs like "A Passage to Bangkok" and "The Twilight Zone" have textures that are perfectly juxtaposed with the title suite, whether matching its metallic intensity or contrasting with it. Both also have titles that suggest exotic locales, mirroring the far-flung setting of Megadon.

It's a sad fact that side two never gets as many accolades as side one, and it never will. That's an easy enough concept to understand, since the "2112" suite is the centerpiece of the record—and no honest person would dispute that. Few lament that Rush did not call their 1976 record *You Didn't Listen Again*.

Still, the five songs collected on side two act as a crucial foil to side one. Furthermore, it has plenty of its own moments of majesty that rival the epic title track's most towering peaks—and it has many of those.

2

On *uDiscoverMusic.com*, writer Brett Milano said the record's flip side "almost sounds like a different band" from the one that just treated us to a complex science fiction fever dream. He said that in contrast to the title track, side two's contents were more relatable to the average earthling.

"['A Passage to Bangkok' and 'The Twilight Zone'] were about the most down-to-earth topics Rush ever addressed," he wrote. "Namely, smoking pot and watching TV."

Lifeson agreed that side two is less elaborate in scope than side one, which may explain why it's often less celebrated. He said that this was a conscious decision, made out of necessity.

"'2112' was so very serious and such an intense piece of work that side two needed to be just a little lighter and a little more fun," he said.

If *you* staged an entire intergalactic war, after all, you might want to follow that up with less conceptually dense stuff, too. Despite invoking the dreaded word "fun," however, Lifeson didn't say any of those five songs were slapdash afterthoughts or lacked substance—quite the opposite, in fact.

"There's some very strong songs on that side," he said. "They tend to be just a little more varied. 'Tears' is very different from 'Lessons' as it is from 'A Passage to Bangkok' or 'The Twilight Zone.'"

While it's tempting to imagine what two full sides of "2112" could sound like, the guitarist said there was no desire on the band's part to go all *Tales from Topographic Oceans* and make the album consist solely of epic tracks. He felt that the existing version of the suite that begins and ends on side one got across what it needed to get across. There was no reason to keep it going on side two.

"I couldn't imagine the story of '2112' being on two sides," he said. "If the whole album was just that spread over 40 minutes, I don't know if it would have worked."

The band clearly made the right decision. While no one can say if a forty-minute version of "2112" would have worked or not, time has proven that the album we ended up with worked brilliantly, all six tracks of it.

I. A PASSAGE TO BANGKOK

Music by Geddy Lee & Alex Lifeson, lyrics by Neil Peart

"A Passage to Bangkok" opens side two of *2112* with an instantly appealing hard rock riff that anchors the song. By now, every person on earth knows that this is a song about smoking pot and all the exotic destinations where one could procure it. By Lifeson's admission, the band quite enjoyed the wacky tobacky at that time; so writing a song about it symbolized the "Write what you know" ethos in action.

"We were average, maybe slightly above-average smokers," he told *PROG* in 2013. "Ged less so. . . . But Neil and I and a few guys in the crew were."

If anything about the song has aged poorly, it's the use of the chop-socky musical motif known familiarly as "The Oriental Riff." This piece of music was used in decades past to invoke the mysterious culture of faraway Asia. If you don't know the riff, listen to the first few seconds of "Turning Japanese" by the New Wave band the Vapors. It also makes an appearance in "Kung Fu Fighting" by Carl Douglas.

While some audiences might take offense to its use today, it's hard to get too worked up about it in this context. It's the product of marijuana-impaired humor, the kind of sophomoric thing you'd expect from a twelve-year-old. Ultimately it's harmless, because it's evident that the humor was not mean-spirited, whatever the impact on listeners today.

CLOCKWISE FROM LEFT Rabid baseball enthusiast and wine collector Geddy Lee at Le Studio in Morin Heights, Quebec in October 1979 during the *Permanent Waves* sessions.

Neil Peart violates the cardinal rule of 1990s indie-rock culture by wearing band merch at his own gig in April 1977.

Justice. Rush gets the full two-page spread treatment they deserve from *Circus* magazine.

PREVIOUS Rush backstage on December 9, 1976, at the Civic Center in Springfield, Massachusetts, during the band's *All the World's a Stage* tour.

"WE SMOKED A LOT OF POT AT THE TIME, AND WE REALLY HAD A GOOD LAUGH OVER THOSE SORTS OF THINGS. WILL IT PASS THE TEST OF TIME? AH, WHO CARES?"

ALEX LIFESON
to *PROG* magazine, 2013

"We smoked a lot of pot at the time, and we really had a good laugh over those sorts of things," Lifeson told *PROG* magazine in 2013. "Will it pass the test of time? Ah, who cares?"

It's not as egregious as the gong sound used in *Sixteen Candles* every time Chinese exchange student Long Duk Dong appears onscreen. But while listeners with more delicate sensibilities may dock the song a few points for using the motif, there's no denying that the other 99 percent of the track is right on point. Lifeson's riff is immediately engaging, and the band probably could have gotten away with just repeating it for four minutes.

The melody and structure are firmly faux-Eastern, although Lee-Lifeson-Peart don't take it as far as Rainbow's "Stargazer," which employs the Munich Symphony Orchestra and the Phrygian dominant scale. Despite its exotic flourishes, Rush keeps "A Passage to Bangkok" firmly in hard rock territory. It's easy to picture 1970s stoners high-fiving each other as Lee sings about where you can buy some puff-puff-pass.

High Times interviewed Lifeson about the song in 2012, and he said it was "very safe to say" the magazine had inspired the song lyrics. The publication would report on exceptional marijuana strains from places such as South America, Mexico, and

Neil Peart in the throes of glorious percussion bacchanalia at London's Hammersmith Odeon, on February 20, 1978.

Alex Lifeson and Neil Peart look on as Geddy Lee plays the Moog. In subsequent years, it would become increasingly difficult to tear the bassist away from these admittedly diverting toys.

Asia. He gave his best guess about how the song that the magazine had inspired came together.

"That song was probably written in a farmhouse, on an acoustic guitar, in front of a little cassette player of some sort," he said. "We would record like that and then go down in the basement and rehearse it."

In 2006, however, he told *Guitar World* that the structure and approach were influenced by the 1975 Led Zeppelin classic "Kashmir."

"'Kashmir' has such a wonderful, exotic Middle Eastern feel to it," he said. "In a roundabout way, 'Kashmir' influenced 'A Passage to Bangkok,' which has a similar sort of odd-tempo arrangement to the verses."

Nicole Biamonte, assistant professor of music theory at the Schulich School of Music at Montreal's McGill University, explained in the 2011 book *Rush and Philosophy: Heart and Mind United* what the guitarist was likely trying to get across.

"He might have meant the heavily syncopated vocal melodies of both songs, in which almost all of the notes fall between the beats rather than on them, creating a stretched-out effect," she said. "Or he might have meant the disjunction between the instrumental riffs and the vocal melodies, which have slower rhythms and irregular phrases that don't quite line up with the riffs."

She said this kind of arrangement helps create an effect on the listener one could describe as almost out-of-body. Neither "Kashmir" nor "A Passage to Bangkok" will cause your soul to hover above your corporeal form, but they create a hypnotic feeling one rarely experiences when listening to traditional FM radio stations.

"In both songs, the result of this rhythmic layering is that the melody seems to float above the accompaniment, disconnected from it," she wrote. "The disconnect between voice and instruments in these two songs is more evocative of a state of mind than a physical place."

In 2013, Richard Bienstock of *Guitar World* asked Lifeson if he or his bandmates had ever experienced "the fragrance of Afghanistan" or any other drug tourism destination name-checked in the song. The guitarist had to disappoint him and say no.

"We might have shared a copy of *High Times* magazine or something and looked at all those places, but that's about it," he said.

He also had the sad duty of disappointing David Bienenstock of *High Times* in 2012. The topic was 1970s-era partying, and he asked if anyone in Rush had ever overindulged in substance abuse to the point of destroying a hotel room like Joe Walsh and so many other rock stars beyond counting.

"Not really, I almost hate to say," he said. "I guess we had our times in those days, but really, we were always in the shadow of the headlining act. If we stayed in the same hotel, we were usually in our rooms looking down the hallway, watching them throw TVs out the window and stuff. That was too expensive a hobby for us. . . . Most times on the road, Neil was reading, and we'd be watching TV or something."

GATES

Donna Halper said that she still enjoys listening to "A Passage to Bangkok" despite never touching marijuana in her entire life. She described it as a fun, entertaining travelogue that contrasted nicely with the menacing title track.

"I would just look at it like, 'Oh, it's vicarious,'" she said. "This gives me, a non-user, the opportunity to pretend, to take on the persona."

Despite enjoying the song, Halper said it never made her the slightest bit curious about trying marijuana, just as one can read *Catcher in the Rye* and not go out and shoot John Lennon.

"Do I ever want to do it? No," she said. "But I can watch a murder mystery and never want to murder anybody either."

II. THE TWILIGHT ZONE

Music by Geddy Lee & Alex Lifeson, lyrics by Neil Peart

On October 10, 1975, the *St. Catharines Standard* reported that a band of young upstarts calling itself Rush had just released their third album, *Caress of Steel*. After saying the songs were too long and featured too many self-indulgent solos, the publication reported a comment made by Lee.

"The new album is dedicated to Rod Serling," he said. "He was one of our great teachers, and at times the band tends to be very Rod-like."

Rod Serling, of course, was the chain-smoking producer of the CBS television series *The Twilight Zone*. Before finding success with it, he had spent years as a frustrated television writer whose scripts were routinely censored.

He would frequently write about politically thorny topics and themes, and sponsors didn't

The holy trinity of Lee-Lifeson-Peart, approaching their promotional duties with the seriousness and solemnity they deserve.

Just as Neil Peart used every single piece of his gigantic drum kit, Alex Lifeson was a skilled enough guitar player to warrant two guitar necks.

want to associate with that kind of thing. This caused his work to be heavily modified, sometimes to the point where an entire script was neutered. He once wrote a script inspired by the murder of Emmett Till, and all the racial subject matter was excised before the episode aired.

He related this situation to television journalist Mike Wallace in 1959. He described it the same way a certain Canadian threesome described their issues with Mercury Records.

"I don't want to have to push for something that I want and have to settle for second best," Serling said. "I don't want to have to compromise all the time, which in essence is what a television writer does if he wants to put on controversial themes."

In that sense, the members of Rush were absolutely Rod-like, so it makes sense that they were fans. The trio routinely bonded over their love for the show and watched it whenever the opportunity to do so arose.

"We felt *The Twilight Zone* was really one of the most creative TV programs available," Lee said in the "Rush: 2112/Moving Pictures" episode of the *Classic Albums* documentary series. "We were always shocked that it even got on the air."

He said that "The Twilight Zone," the band's tribute to the program, was the last song written for *2112*. Despite dedicating their previous album to the guy already, they had affection and respect to spare for Rod Serling, and coming up with a song in his honor was not burdensome in any way.

"We wrote 'The Twilight Zone' spontaneously in the studio," he said in *MusicRadar.com* in 2016. Two episodes of the series provide the source material for the lyrics, "Will the Real Martian Please Stand Up?" and "Stopover in a Quiet Town."

The latter is a cautionary tale about the perils of impaired driving. The main characters wake up from the previous night's alcoholic stupor as miniaturized, pet versions of human beings belonging to a giant child.

"If you drink, don't drive," he said. "And if your wife has had a couple, she shouldn't drive either. You both might just wind up with a whale of a headache in a deserted village in *The Twilight Zone*."

As far as the music goes, "The Twilight Zone" is a gem, with stellar guitar playing throughout. The verses give story synopses and play out against a light shuffle beat. It shifts into straight time for the choruses, which are exquisitely arranged and feature light acoustic picking. Lee performs a delicate, keening vocal, backed by his own whispering in the background.

After some thoughtful, restrained guitar leads and atmospheric playing from Lee and Peart, the plane glides to a gentle landing after around three and a half minutes. The song functions as a welcome breather after the bombast on side one.

Lifeson said he was particularly pleased with the solo. It was hardly the most complicated or technical thing he would ever play, but it has a quality that Rush was not often lauded for at the time—restraint.

"There's something just being held back," he said. "Something is dangerous about it, just like in every episode of *The Twilight Zone*, there's something dangerous and unexpected. . . . When you watched any episode, you always felt like something is going to happen."

2112 co-producer Terry Brown told *PROG* that he had always loved the track. He said it was not just a high point of the record but one of his favorite things the trio had ever recorded.

"'The Twilight Zone' is a little gem with a very strong lead guitar motif from Alex," he said, "Ged's verse vocals up in the stratosphere and then the chorus slipping into an eerie flanged vocal that's in the 'zone.' It's all held together by Neil's very concise, driving percussion, closing with the airy guitar solo which makes this one of my favorite Rush tunes."

In 2007, author Stewart T. Stanyard wrote his own tribute to the television show, a behind-the-scenes look called *Dimensions Behind the Twilight Zone: A Backstage Tribute to Television's Groundbreaking Series*. Appropriately, Peart wrote the foreword, which he called "Magic Realism Comes to the Suburbs." He detailed the effect the show had on him both as a child and as a working musician.

He said that the program had been an early example of magic realism, a literary genre that emerged in the 1960s from the pens of various Latin American authors. *One Hundred Years of Solitude* by Gabriel García Márquez is one of the most famous examples of the genre, but its 1967 vintage means *The Twilight Zone* beat it to the punch and got there first. Peart said Serling had single-handedly invented the genre of magic realism, despite the fact that it's considered a purely literary movement today.

"[Serling's] screenplays were always rich in carefully drawn details of background and character, whether the story was set in the familiar world of the suburbs, a typical contemporary background like the Old West, or an imaginary planet. But in the end, there was always a supernatural twist, sometimes ironic, sometimes thought-provoking, sometimes chilling."

Peart said the show's depth set it apart it from other contemporary science fiction fare, such as *The Outer Limits* or *The Day the Earth Stood Still*. As beloved as that stuff is, the drummer said that Serling's scripts always set the bar higher, and he was happy to see that decades later, the show's high quality and engrossing situations still had as much power to draw viewers as ever.

"Almost 30 years later, and 40 years after the series was aired, it is wonderful to know that *The Twilight Zone* continues to be celebrated and enjoyed, as this book proves," he said. "I am very happy to see the legacy of Rod Serling and his collaborators live on."

III. LESSONS

Music by and lyrics by Alex Lifeson

"Lessons" is one of two songs on *2112* with music and lyrics written entirely by a single band member. That song—and the Lee-penned "Tears"—represented the first two times this had ever occurred in Rush history, and it never happened again. Fittingly, Lifeson played slide guitar for the first time on a Rush album on this same song, and that never happened again, either.

It starts with bright acoustic guitars that vaguely recall the "Presentation" movement of "2112," albeit at a slightly quicker tempo. It's a sunny 1970s feel-good pop song that would not sound out of place emanating from the P.A. in the Walgreens toothpaste aisle. Then it goes *way* harder during the chorus, affording Peart the opportunity to execute some insane fills every time Lee pauses between lines.

During the chorus, Lee sings, "You didn't listen again," backed by a Lifeson lead guitar that doubles the vocal melody, playing in unison with it. The effect is one of discordant exasperation, the kind one hears from a teenager pushing back against Mom and Dad.

In fact, it sort of recalls Lifeson's argument with his parents in *Come on Children*. It's almost as though Lee is singing it to Nenad and Melanija Živojinović on Lifeson's behalf, while the guitarist reinforces the melody in the background.

Whatever the song's inspiration, it remains one of a handful of times when the guitarist tried to write lyrics for a Rush album. It wasn't a horrible ordeal for him, but he vastly preferred the role of guitar player and was happier practicing scales than engaging in wordsmithery. He didn't hate it, but it wasn't for him, and he was glad that Peart pretty much had all that covered.

"I can't say that I'm comfortable writing lyrics," Lifeson told *Rolling Stone* in 2016. "It doesn't flow for me the way I would like it to."

"Lessons" fades out slowly, and it feels like they could have easily returned for another verse and chorus without anyone minding. They play it out on an extended guitar solo instead.

Overall, it's a strong tune, and the album is well served by having it on side two for mood, pacing, and texture. Still, it seems to be missing a little something—they pull it off competently, but this type of cheerful, major-key acoustic outing would be revisited and perfected as "Cinderella Man" on their next album, *A Farewell to Kings*. They did a fine job with "Lessons," but they nailed it on "Cinderella Man."

Rush never performed "Lessons" live, most likely because performing "Passage to Bangkok," "Something for Nothing," and the "2112" suite just took up so much room on the set list back then that there wasn't time for any other material from the record. Sadly, it slipped through the cracks, and over the years, it never exceeded its deep cut status. The ultimate irony is that if it had appeared on *Caress of Steel* instead of *2112*, it could well have been exactly the single Mercury wanted the band to deliver in 1975.

How does the song fare among contemporary audiences? In 2018, *Vice* writer Josh Terry played *2112* in its entirety for Dylan Baldi, singer and songwriter for the indie rock band Cloud Nothings. He had been aware of Rush thanks to his parents, big fans who played their music with great regularity as he was growing up. He had never sat down with the album before, so he gave all thirty-nine minutes his undivided attention.

Baldi made numerous insightful observations as he listened. He praised Lee's vocal delivery during the "Temples of Syrinx" movement of the "2112" suite, and for once, there was no comparison of Lee's singing voice to that of Led Zeppelin's golden god, Robert Plant.

"He has a good voice," Baldi said. "He sounds like Pat Benatar."

Alex Lifeson surrounded by his numerous beloved axes backstage during the *All the World's a Stage* tour, hopefully making Nenad and Melanija Živojinović feel at ease with his decision to pursue music full-time.

Despite its reputation as a lesser highlight of *2112*, Baldi had a very positive reaction to "Lessons." He described it as "really tight," and it made him curious if this Alex Lifeson character had ever written any other songs besides this one.

"I might like him more as a songwriter just from this," he said while consulting the Internet for factoids about the Rush guitarist. "He's been married since 1975 to the same person. A family guitarist. Right on. I'm looking him up right now. He's a licensed pilot and owns a bar in Toronto called the Orbit Room."

Normally, Lifeson is acclaimed for his guitar playing. His worth as a songwriter is a much less discussed topic among Rush fans, which also goes for Lee. He has graced the covers of bass

“I CAN’T SAY THAT I’M COMFORTABLE WRITING LYRICS; IT DOESN’T FLOW FOR ME THE WAY I WOULD LIKE IT TO.”

ALEX LIFESON, to *Rolling Stone,* 2016

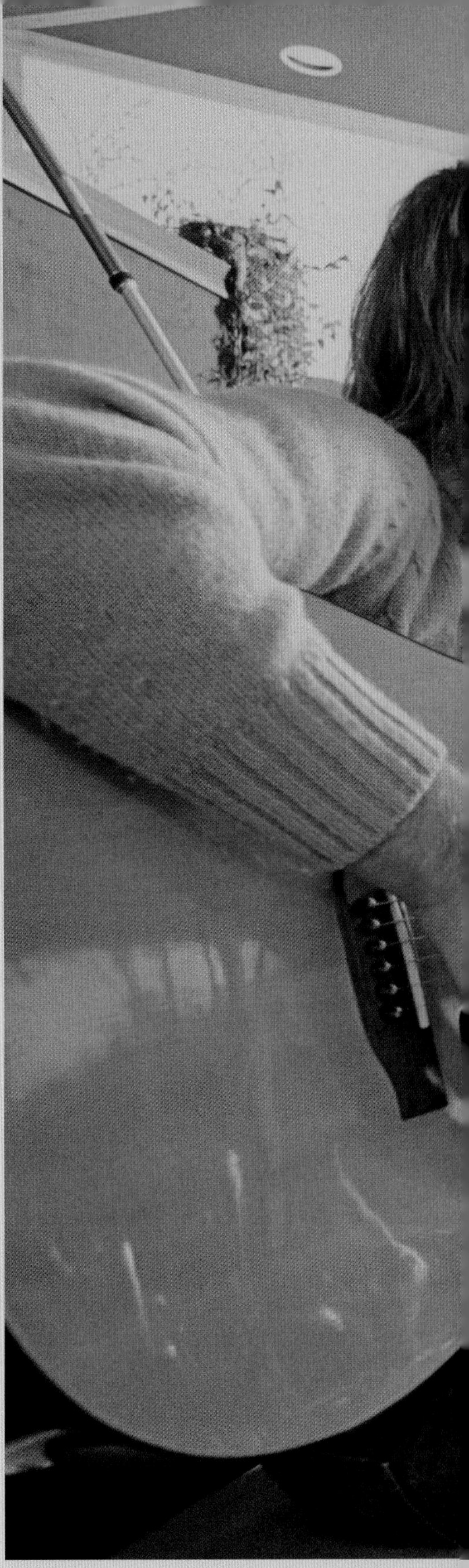

“What the hell does ‘the clouds prepare for battle’ mean?” Lifeson, Peart, and Lee have a pow-wow during the October 1979 *Permanent Waves* sessions at Le Studio in Morin Heights, Quebec.

"Anonymous, 2112"

One feature of *2112* that's taken a hit in the digital age is its album cover. What was once a twelve-inch image was reduced to a fraction of that size on CD booklets.

2112's front cover is visually striking enough to cut through even when Spotify reduces it to the size of a postage stamp. Unfortunately, the finer points of the artwork were compromised in the process, if not eliminated, which ultimately detracts from the full effect of the record for the listener. To truly take in *2112* as intended, every feature of the cover has to be there, including all the fine print, which is exactly how the Anonymous narrator's journal is rendered. It's there if you look for it, but if you don't have the vinyl, it's going to take some doing on your part.

The journal is one of the finer details on the record jacket, and it really got the shaft when album covers became CD covers. Excerpts from the narrator's journal appear in various places on the cover, but that's hard to pick out if you don't have the full version of the artwork that houses the vinyl. The text block beneath the oft-derided band photo is legible on the back of the LP jacket, but it's next to impossible to decipher on a CD booklet. Excerpts also accompany the lyrics of "2112," and again, if you have the gatefold LP cover, you can see them all. If you don't, then you can't.

The journal entries are not essential to the "2112" suite's plot and provide next to nothing in the way of exposition. What we hear emanating from the speakers tells us the story in its entirety. Regardless, the excerpts give depth and color that couldn't be crammed into the lyrics.

The printed lyrics to "The Temples of Syrinx" are preceded by an excerpt in which the narrator describes his life prior to discovering an ancient guitar.

". . . The massive grey walls of the Temples rise from the Heart of every Federation city. . . . Our books, our music, our work and play are all looked after by the benevolent wisdom of the priests. . . ."

A similar preamble precedes the lyrics to each movement, all attributed to "Anonymous, 2112." Through these passages, the listener learns a little more about life in Megadon.

The city's residents watch "Templevision" and read the "Temple Paper." There are two moons, and the moons throughout the Solar Federation are all that remain of planets that perished in the intergalactic war of 2062.

The excerpts shed a little more light on Megadon's status as a futuristic Jonestown. Father Brown runs it, and when the narrator considers presenting the guitar, he believes Brown and all the other priests will be wise and well-intended in receiving it. Unfortunately, it's Father Brown who not only rejects it but destroys it, a detail not included in the lyrics.

"I watched in shock and horror as Father Brown ground my precious instrument to splinters beneath his feet," the journal says.

The remainder of the journal goes into more detail about the narrator's eventual emotional unraveling. Prose can do that. It can get into whatever detail it wants for as long as it wants, a luxury that doesn't exist when joining lyrics to music. The narrator's decision to end his life gets a couple of sentences of written development that the musical structure doesn't permit. Peart keeps the entries economical and free of Proustian paragraphs about vicissitudes, so while it doesn't go into depth, it adds a little something to the listening experience.

In 2018, when *Vice* reporter Josh Terry played *2112* for Dylan Baldi of Cloud Nothings, he was given the LP version to listen to. This allowed him to experience the album cover as intended, in all its prose-enhanced splendor. Eventually, he asked the question a lot of Rush fans in 1976 probably asked when reading those same journal entries for the first time: What's the point of these excerpts if they never come up in the lyrics?

"Background and color," Terry explained. "It's kind of nerdy but I can totally see how people got obsessed over it. It's badass escapism and they really created their own world in a 20-minute song."

While vinyl records are unlikely to become as popular with present-day consumers as they were in the 1970s, a decent number of young people have begun embracing the format, many for a simple reason—all the extra goodies the naked eye can pick out on a double-panel gatefold.

While many a graybeard may read this and rejoice that Boomer artifacts like record covers are being embraced by their grandchildren, they should temper their glee. Baldi signed off with a statement about concept albums that's both inspiring and heartbreaking to those emotionally invested in the art form. It will live on, but not necessarily in the form they prefer.

"Concept albums or songs like this are always a good idea," Baldi said. "I saw Taylor Swift pretty recently and her latest album is essentially a concept record."

The narrator's journal entries help flesh out *2112* and are part of what the group intended. That vision, which Rush would fight for their entire career, was compromised by the shrinking of album artwork for the compact disc age, just as surely as the first CD edition of *All the World's a Stage* compromised the artist's vision by omitting the last song so it could fit on a single disc.

For listeners who have heard the music but could never explore its visual intricacies, it's worth tracking down a copy of *2112* on vinyl so the listening experience can be taken in as intended. The music is good enough that you can get by without it, but that doesn't mean you should.

The Story of "2112"

In the year 2062, a galaxy-wide war results in the union of all planets under the rule of the Red Star of the Solar Federation. The world is controlled by computers, called Temples, which determine all reading matter, songs, pictures . . . everything connected with life during the year 2112 ("The Temples of Syrinx").

In the midst of this assembly line living, a man discovers what was once known years before as a guitar ("Discovery"). The man begins to pluck the strings and turn the knobs, discovering that he can make his own music — a music much different than that of the Temples. He rushes to tell the priests of his discovery, ("Presentation") but to the man's dismay, the priests dismiss the instrument, saying it doesn't fit the plan of the Solar Federation.

The man returns to the cave in which he found the guitar and, during a dream, is led by an oracle to a land of incredible beauty and serenity ("Oracle: A Dream"). Upon awakening, he can not believe it was a dream — the beauty was so real.

He remains in the save for several days, becoming more and more depressed with each passing hour ("Soliloquy"). The man decides he can not go on as part of the Federation and takes his life to move on to a better one. As he dies, another planetary battle begins ("Grand Finale") with the outcome to be determined in the mind of the listener.

SIDE ONE

"2112"
I Overture
II The Temples of Syrinx
III Discovery
IV Presentation
V Oracle: The Dream
VI Soliloquy
VII Grand Finale

SIDE TWO

A Passage To Bangkok
The Twilight Zone
Lessons
Tears
Something For Nothing

Produced by Rush and Terry Brown

The story of the "2112" suite as described in the tour program for Rush's three-night engagement at Toronto's Massey Hall in June 1976.

player magazines beyond number, but few talk about his songwriting. Rush are perceived by many as a band of highly technical musicians who represent the elite in their field, but with the exception of Peart's lyrics, songwriting in general is not a primary topic of discussion among fans, even though they love all the songs.

This may be because listeners view the music written for Rush as a democratic effort, a collective endeavor distributed evenly among band members. While there are still scads of Beatle fans proclaiming John Lennon a better songwriter than Paul McCartney and vice versa, one is highly unlikely to ever encounter a Rush fan who asks, "Who's a better songwriter, Geddy or Alex?"

IV. TEARS

Music and lyrics by Geddy Lee

"Tears" is Lee's entry in the "Write a whole song by yourself for *2112*" sweepstakes. It's an achingly beautiful ballad, and there had been nothing like it in the Rush catalog up to that point. "Rivendell" and "In the End" had ended *Fly by Night* on a mellow and introspective note a year prior, but "Tears" took the sound of those songs and took them many steps further into a bolder and more progressive direction.

It's the type of song that Lifeson said Lee is inherently inclined to compose.

"'Tears' is so typical of the kind of stuff that he likes to write and do, even today," he said. ""He likes those more ballad-y pieces that are emotive and sweet. I'm the dirty, heavy guy."

Geddy Lee makes himself at home backstage at London's Hammersmith Odeon on February 19, 1978, during the *A Farewell to Kings* tour.

"Tears" expands upon all previous Rush songs by using instrumentation outside the power trio guitar-bass-drums arsenal. Specifically, it uses Mellotron backing, which was arranged and performed by illustrator Hugh Syme.

In *uDiscoverMusic.com*, Brett Milano likened it to the mellower mid-1970s offerings of Tony Iommi, Geezer Butler, Bill Ward, and the Prince of Darkness.

"['Tears'] sounds more like a Black Sabbath ballad (see 'Solitude' or 'Changes') than anything else by Rush," he said.

The comparison to the keyboard-soaked "Changes" is particularly apt. No matter who you compare it to, however, it's next to impossible to hear a Mellotron and not immediately draw comparisons to "The Court of the Crimson King."

"The gentleman that does all our album covers is called Hugh Syme, and it's actually him playing Mellotron here," Lee told *MusicRadar.com* in 2016. "Mellotrons are very unique-sounding; they sound sort of electric, but also kind of stringy, they have this real resin-y sound to them, which is very cool and unique to that period."

Syme's contribution to "Tears" came about as the result of an offhand comment. He was in the studio during the *2112* sessions as the song was being crafted, and he mentioned that it would be nice if someone enhanced it with some other sounds. As it turned out, Syme was someone.

"I just happened to say, 'I'd like to hear some really nice flute or Mellotron,'" he said. "Terry said, 'Have at it.' So I went down the hall for three hours and worked up the parts for that song. It was an unwitting and unplanned kind of invitation."

BELOW A full-page advertisement run by the music magazine *Sounds* for *2112*.

RIGHT Neil Peart *sans* handlebar 'stache and *avec* "Starman" logo on his double-bass drums at Bingley Hall in Staffordshire, England, on September 21, 1979.

When he came back, the parts he had written were immediately accepted. There were no follow-up questions, additional input, or criticisms. They took the arrangement as is.

"There was not one comment saying, 'Well, can we try this?' I think they just dug what they heard," he said.

He added that the band's receptivity to his contribution was as enthusiastic as it was in part because it introduced a new element into the Rush sound. Until then, they had followed the Grand Funk Railroad template and relied on a power trio sound in all its unrefined glory. The Mellotron part on "Tears" represented a first true foray into broadening their instrumental vocabulary. Everyone in the studio was excited by it.

"It was very early in the band's experience with textures beyond bass, drums, and guitar," he said. "It was a welcome and refreshing sound to them."

He said he had been very surprised by the song's delicacy, something he hadn't expected from the band at that point.

"'Tears' was one of the more exposed and intimate songs I've ever heard from Geddy," Syme said.

There was a reason for that. The subject matter, it turned out, was a bit of a slice of life for Lee. Donna Halper said life on the road was difficult for the bassist, and balancing the touring musician's demanding schedule and pressures with married life was difficult. He loved to play every night in the arenas of the world, but he loved his wife, too, and wanted to be home with her. The distance could be hard to endure sometimes.

"Let's be honest, you're away most of the time," she said. "You're here, your spouse is there, and maybe you've got kids, maybe you miss them. Maybe you wish they were around, and they're not. He loved Nancy, and he really did want to be there, but he did love his music too, and he wanted to try to find a balance."

BELOW Rush at Le Studio in Morin Heights, Quebec, in October 1979 during the *Permanent Waves* recording sessions.

RIGHT, TOP Geddy Lee at the stage door entrance of the Odeon in Birmingham, England, on February 12, 1978, during the *A Farewell to Kings* tour.

RIGHT, BELOW A commemorative illustration of Neil Peart inspired by the style of the *2112* LP with the January 7, 2020, date of his passing.

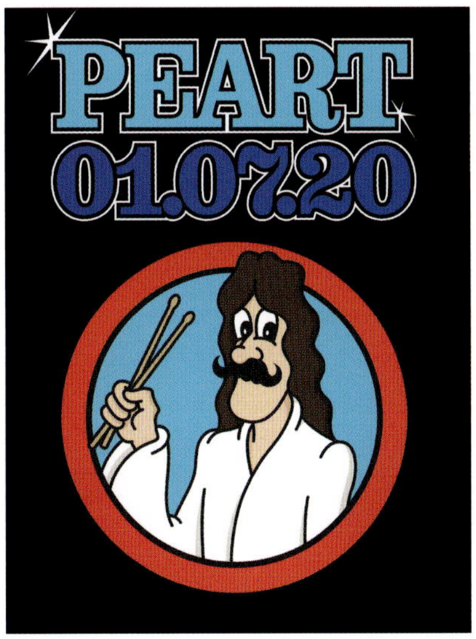

Perhaps driven by the genuine sorrow Lee was feeling, "Tears" comes through as an unusually emotional and sincere song for this group, which had never recorded anything this personal before. It also could have been a perfect single for *Caress of Steel*, just like "Lessons."

Honestly, it's strange that it's not a more highly regarded song by fans. It hits all the right notes in terms of melody and performance, and it feels like the band is sharing a moment of genuine intimacy and vulnerability with the listener. It feels real.

The Mellotron used on "Tears" is an unobtrusive, background feature of the arrangement that gives the song added color. After this, Rush would go nuts and begin festooning their music with all kinds of electronic gadgets and doohickeys.

This was not always welcomed by every fan, particularly when it culminated in albums like *Power Windows* and *Hold Your Fire*, in which every song is so drenched in synthesizer padding that it can obscure the individual musicians' performances. But on *2112*, the keyboard enhanced the power trio, not the other way around.

"Keys were quite new to them and having them become a part of their music was refreshing, maybe even a little bit exciting for all of us," Syme said. "To this day, I feel privileged and grateful for having had that opportunity."

V. SOMETHING FOR NOTHING

Music by Geddy Lee & Alex Lifeson, lyrics by Neil Peart

Upon reaching adulthood, most of us internalize a valuable and timeless life lesson. Namely, if you spend all day every day eating Pop-Tarts, doing bong rips, and playing *Project Zomboid*, you are highly unlikely to achieve your dreams. Sure, anything can happen, and who knows? Maybe the ceiling will open up and start showering you with free money as your reward for doing absolutely nothing, but it's not likely.

At some point, if you want anything to happen, you have to get up.

"Something for Nothing," the fifth and final track on side two of *2112*, is a song about self-determination with a simple theme: If you want something, you must go out and make it a reality. It must be you, and it can only be you. No one will do it for you, and no one will hand it to you. For better or worse, you're on your own.

In his 2004 book *Traveling Music: The Soundtrack to My Life and Times*, Peart said he was inspired to write the song's lyrics in Los Angeles in the mid-1970s. On the way to the Shrine Auditorium, he saw graffiti spray-painted on a wall saying, "Freedom isn't free." Peart's adapted lyric became, "You can't have freedom for free."

He explained that in his view, freedom wasn't only about the fun stuff. It isn't about following every impulse, unchecked, with no regard for the consequences. If anything, freedom can be as isolating as it is liberating. Most of us think of it as freedom from responsibilities and life's worries, but there's another side to it—you can also be free of human connection, community, and support. It cuts both ways.

"All those paeans to American restlessness and the American road carried a tinge of wistfulness," he wrote. "An acknowledgment of the hardships of the vagrant life, the notion that wanderlust could be involuntary, exile as much as freedom, and indeed, the understanding that freedom wasn't free."

Lee described the song as "our balls-to-the-wall rocker" in *MusicRadar.com* in 2016. He said it's a song about individual will, tying it back to the central theme of "2112." If *2112* can be said to be a concept album, then that's the concept, and the song ties back to it.

"I guess it's different to the rest of side two because it's a song that does relate to the first side, and very much so," he said.

The song is a masterpiece, and that's not hyperbole. It's the final response to side one as well as a restatement of its theme, which boils down to "You and only you must go do the thing," whether it's scaling Mount Everest or presenting the Priests with an ancient guitar. It articulates all of that very clearly in a tidy four minutes, yet somehow, it still manages to be equally as epic and sprawling as "2112."

Since "Something for Nothing" is not formally attached to the concept piece on side one, it can get its point across in a clearer and more concise way than the title track. It also provides a blueprint to the listener who's freaked out by the implications of the "2112" story. "Something for Nothing" is, in many ways, a guidebook for avoiding the Anonymous narrator's fate.

The structure is a little unusual in that the guitar solo comes right after the first verse and chorus. It's not a radical approach to songwriting, but it's a little different nonetheless from where guitar solos were typically situated in the hard rock songs of 1976. Despite that, you don't notice a missing second verse and chorus at all. Nothing seems out of place, and everything feels like it's exactly where it should be.

After the solo, the instruments briefly drop out, and then Lee sings the personal manifesto part of the song. Telling us that "what you live

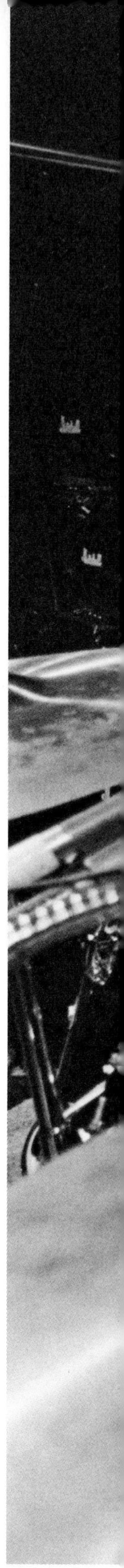

RIGHT Take that! Neil Peart at Chicago's Aragon Ballroom on May 20, 1977, showing all lesser drummers how it's supposed to be done.

ABOVE Geddy Lee plucks at his Rickenbacker 4001 while wailing at London's Hammersmith Odeon on February 20, 1978.

RIGHT Get lost, Dolby Atmos! Amscray, 5.1 surround mixes! Presenting Rush's *2112* the way it was meant to be heard: on the most nonsensical format of the 1970s, the 8-track tape!

is your own story" reinforces the observation that you don't need to be a historical figure to lead a life of significance. You can be anybody, and whatever you're doing matters, as long as it originates from you and comes from a sincere place. But no one is going to go out to the store and return with shopping bags full of your wildest dreams realized. You have to go out there and build your life yourself.

If you can listen to those lyrics and internalize them, they're very inspiring. If you're a Burger King fry cook, the lyrics propose that even that has a sort of nobility, because you're the one doing it. That nobility is, in turn, transferrable to everything else you own, do, love, and live.

According to the 1999 book *Mystic Rhythms: The Philosophical Vision of Rush*, this philosophy has a biblical underpinning. The book cites the Lord's Prayer, which closes with, "For thine is the kingdom, and the power, and the glory, forever."

"Here the phrases are reapplied: you are to seek your own kingdom, your own glory, your own power, your own story," the book said.

"Something for Nothing" is one of the best songs the band ever recorded, and it's as much a statement of purpose as the title track. If "2112" is an ambitious statement about nonconformity, "Something for Nothing" proposes that you can refuse to fit in if you want. Honestly, if you listen to the "What you own . . ." section of the song and you're not inspired by it, call 911 immediately. You need medical attention.

It would be hard to come up with a stronger statement of independence than *2112*'s closing track. The band had their vision and resolved to get behind it and fight for it, do or die. It stood a good chance of being a quixotic kamikaze mission, but it was the leap of faith the band wanted to take.

"I think at the very end of it we believed that this was our protest record," Lifeson said. "That was the statement that we wanted to make clear. What you

An advertisement for *2112* in the April 10, 1976, issue of *RPM* announces the gold certification of 1975's *Fly by Night* LP and says the 1976 album is poised "to capture the imagination of an already spellbound following."

make is who you are and you have to stand on your principles and your own personal integrity."

In 2016, the guitarist said that "Something for Nothing" showed Peart taking Ayn Rand's writing to heart, but mainly as it pertained to self-determination and nonconformity. If there were other aspects of her writing that he considered ideal subject matter for future compositions, he kept it to himself.

"What Neil found in [Ayn Rand's] writing was not so much about her libertarian views," he said. "What he's always got from her writing is that it's about the power of the individual, to do great things, to rely on yourself, nobody's there to do anything for you. You have to do it on your own, you have to craft what you want to do, and be the best that you can."

SECTOR THREE

SECTOR
SECTOR
SECTOR

Rush delivers the goods during the *All the World's*

WARNING

"NEIL'S NEON NIGHTMARE"

ONCE *2112* WAS RECORDED, MIXED, AND DELIVERED, there was little left to do but wait for the reaction. The first one came from the record company, who had been promised a record full of radio-friendly hits. While some of what's on side two could have qualified for that, the label executives had to listen to all twenty minutes of the "2112" suite to get to any of it.

In 2013, Lee told *PROG* that when the record company finally got to hear the record, the reception was less than stellar.

"They didn't like *2112* when we played it for them," the bassist said, "I remember that plainly, and it was not a good moment. We loved the album, but when we played it for those guys, it felt like it was about two hours long."

Co-manager Ray Danniels did not respond in a way that was to Lee's liking either. They had dispatched him to Mercury Records during the *2112* sessions to reassure the label that the new record would be a surefire pop juggernaut. Now, here they were, with the very record itself spinning right in front of them, and no hit materialized.

"Ray, our manager, his face was blank," the bassist said. "We were sweating. We didn't understand why *Caress of Steel* had failed so badly, so we had no reason to believe that *2112* would be any different. And the response from the company and management was no cause for optimism."

Donna Halper remembered her Mercury colleagues' initial reaction to *2112*. A&R executive Cliff Burnstein loved it, but otherwise the feeling at the label was that the band had delivered another record that would be as hard to promote as *Caress of Steel*.

"BETTER YET IS SIDE TWO, WHERE THE FIVE SINGLE ENTRIES RADIATE ENERGY LIKE PULSARS."

PIERRE-RENÉ NOTH in the *Milwaukee Journal*, 1976

ABOVE Blimey! Geddy Lee at Bingley Hall in Staffordshire, England, on September 21, 1979, enjoying the new-found British popularity that resulted from a journalist calling them crypto-fascists.

PREVIOUS Rush outside their tour bus, somewhere in Illinois in May 1977. It was month ten of the *All the World's a Stage* tour, with one more to go.

"My recollection is the people at the label were like, 'Ew, this is not what we had in mind,'" she said.

It could have ended right there. Many record companies will cut their losses and deny promotion to an album they don't believe will sell. Others will not even release it at all in the first place. Mercury, to their credit, got behind *2112*. The label released a press kit that gave no indication whatsoever of the reception the record had gotten from them.

"The just-released *2112* is a natural progression from *Caress of Steel*," the press kit said. "One side is a futuristic tale of life on another planet where individuality and creativity have been stamped out, with computers controlling everything. The other side contains conventional songs. Both sides carry the Rush trademark of hard rock. . . . there is little doubt that 1976 will be a breakout for the group in the entire U.S. market."

Mercury offered fans the tantalizing opportunity to break bread with the trio in a promotion called "Dine with Rush," and frankly, it didn't sound half bad.

"Mercury recording artists, Rush, enjoyed an SRO crowd during their recent Hamilton Place concert, with Polydor's promo rep, Bob Ansell, teaming up with CKOC in a pool of promotional resources for a grand prize giveaway of an autographed Rush LP library, dinner with the band and front row seats for the concert," *RPM Weekly* reported on March 6, 1976.

When the critics finally got their hands on *2112*, their responses were varied. Some gave the band points for expanding their sound and vision, while others were the kind of gratuitously obnoxious bilge that the band had come to expect by that point.

On March 24, 1976, Pierre-René Noth wrote in the *Milwaukee Journal* that the trio's music was "a methadone dose for Led Zeppelin addicts." Still, he conceded that the "2112" suite worked "fairly well," and he had even better things to say about the flip side.

"Better yet is side two, where the five single entries radiate energy like pulsars," he wrote.

A few days later, on March 27, 1976, the *Meriden (CT) Record & Journal* said in its "Big Daddy's Album Review" section that Boston rockers Aerosmith could now step aside. Rush, their "successor," had rendered the Toxic Twins obsolete.

After a few sentences attempting to summarize the "2112" backstory, the *Record & Journal* said a guitar is found by a "curious young punk," lending further credence to the assertion that Rush was a punk rock band. While the publication predictably cited Lee's "uncanny vocal resemblance to Robert Plant," he ultimately said the record worked.

"Unlike some concept albums that get bogged down in their own dogma, '2112' really rocks," it said. "This album should be at the top of any hard rock shopping list."

Not every publication viewed the album as charitably. On April 11, 1976, Jim Shaw of the *Shreveport (LA) Times* opined that the biggest problem with *2112* was "2112."

"The plot is one expansive cliché," Shaw wrote. "Rush would do well to leave this type of composition to other groups capable of producing original pieces, e.g. Emerson, Lake, and Palmer's 'Karn Evil 9, 3rd Impression.' . . . *2112* is a fair album that could have been better if someone had turned the death ray on Rush's trite vision of the future."

On April 24, 1976, the *Windsor (Ontario) Star* said that while *2112* was an improvement over the "turgid" *Caress of Steel*, that darn singer of theirs kept ruining the songs.

"One half of the album is 'concept,' and the only thing wrong with the concept is that Geddy Lee's banshee yowl of a voice completely pulverizes the lyrics," the publication said, while reserving some goodwill for side two, saying it features "Geddy singing in his 'real' voice."

Many publications that gave the album mixed reviews still gave high marks to the group's instrumental proficiency. Indeed, even the band's most committed haters had to grudgingly concede that the members of Rush could play very well.

The *Saskatoon (Sask.) Star-Phoenix* was not one of them. On April 30, 1976, the publication gave the group a bizarrely hostile review. Many reviews of Rush albums were just glorified lists of grievances, and this one was no different.

"Canada's heavy of heavy have another musical offering if one can call it that," the publication said. "They try to make their lyrics intellectual, hoping to seduce listeners with their pretentious mysticism."

Many publications of the era simply could not resist giving Lee grief for his singing voice. The *Star-Phoenix* was only too happy to pile on in assessing his capabilities.

"The formula for this disc seems to be one part soft rock, one part hard, and then one part eardrum-piercing screeches by vocalist Geddy Lee," the publication said. "The music goes down well when it is restrained and Lee is singing without sounding like someone in pain. However, for every few soft bars, there is an onslaught of heavy metal screeching. In comparison, water torture and dentist drills would be a delight."

The review concluded that the band was being too clever for its own good. Maybe the band could get by playing stupid three-chord rock at the volume of a jet engine, but clearly, they were too intellectually stunted to pull off anything more complicated than that.

"If they had concentrated on heavy rock, they might've stood a chance," the review said. "But they want to be rock poets as well as a heavy metal band, and the two won't combine. They do not go beyond rehashing well-worn rock."

Not all of the critics had their knives out. On May 21, 1976, the *Fort Worth Star-Telegram* said the "2112" suite was "above average." It was nice to see a few members of the journalistic class give them a little credit, particularly when compared to many of the antagonistic reviews the band frequently suffered at the time.

"While they may be only three, [Rush] generate enough energy for a band four times their size," the *Star-Telegram* said. "The compositions flow evenly through peaks and valleys of supercharged rock, and although hard rock seems to be on the wane, Rush carries it off in fine fashion. . . . Side two is made up of individual tunes. Standouts here include the flighty 'A Passage to Bangkok' and 'Lessons,' a well-balanced effort that might go as a single."

Unfortunately, even some people who had previously been sympathetic to Rush didn't care for *2112*. Jeffrey Morgan, writing under the name "Machine Rock," wrote a piece about the band for *Cheap Thrills* in 1977. While he gave high marks to their self-titled 1974 debut (". . . it's a killer . . ."), *Fly by Night* (". . . pulse-pounders . . ."), and *Caress of Steel* (". . . perfectly combines both worlds of HM Madness and light, sensitive probings . . ."), he was considerably less charitable to *2112*.

"I hate this one," he wrote. "I think it's wretched. . . . I could've written better—and have!"

That kind of statement tends to be definitive, and elaborating on it poses challenges. Morgan, on the other hand, just kept on handing out insults as if his review was going to be read at the Comedy Central Roast of *2112*.

"*2112* is a glossy piece of garbage that fails because it's so goddamned juvenile it has to be heard to be believed," he said. "Concept albums require mature thought processes and finished products. *2112* has neither. Don't ask me for specifics 'cause I'm not going to give you any—they're not worth my time. Let's just say that the boys bit off more than they could chew and leave it at that, O.K.?"

Meanwhile, some critics, such as Dan Nooger of *Circus*, were able to appreciate the record for what it was. He called the "2112" suite "Neil's neon nightmare," a description that suggested he understood what the band was trying to get across. He added that the band had come a long way since "In the Mood."

"'2112' features some significant Mellotron meanderings and amazingly eccentric lyrics," he said. "Pretty deep stuff for an ex-bar band whose prosody has never been much more ambitious than 'You're making me crazy the way you roll them eyes.'"

On average, the mainstream press reception to *2112* upon its release ranged from "I hate this one" to "above average," approximately a two-star rating out of five. Between that and the label's response upon hearing the record for the first time, there seemed scant reason for Rush to celebrate.

Nonetheless, it was time to take *2112* on tour.

Rush enjoy the quiet sanctity of their bus on the *All the World's a Stage* tour. The promotional trek lasted almost a full year, so they really got used to that interior.

"POPPING THE CASH REGISTER OPEN"

2

WHILE CRITICS MAY HAVE BEEN LARGELY STAND-OFFISH in their appraisal of *2112*, their opinion doesn't count. Why? Because they all got review copies of the album for free.

How did it go over with the fans and general record buyers? What did the people think after dipping into their discretionary income to buy a copy?

The short version is that they liked it, and the friends they played it for liked it, too. Those people would, in turn, buy a copy of their own, which they would play for other people, who also got on board. The record company promoted the album as it was supposed to, and there had been a smattering of decent reviews, but none of that was as powerful a promotion tool as word-of-mouth among the fans. No amount of press releases can accomplish what the fans can accomplish just by playing their favorite records for friends.

The LP of *2112* sold one hundred thousand copies in its first month of release. It eventually reached the #5 spot on Canadian charts and reached the top 100 on the U.S. *Billboard* charts, eventually reaching its peak at #61.

The Recording Industry Association of America (RIAA) certified *2112* Gold on November 16, 1977, then triple Platinum in 1995, denoting three million copies sold.

The record-buying public was Rush's saving grace. The larger music industry and the rock press may have been dismissive of them, but street-level music fans embraced them and stayed loyal to them.

In 2016, Lifeson told *Rolling Stone* that he remembered *2112* steadily gaining popularity as the tour continued. It took a little time, but the commercial performance of the record defied Mercury Records' worst fears. It was selling, and no hit single had made it happen. It was a purely organic thing.

"It took about a year to go gold," he said. "So it was a slow but progressive evolution. Once it got to that point where it really started to take off, there was word of mouth and more interest in the band, and all of those things came together to make a movement. That really bought our independence from the record company."

Donna Halper already knew some rock bands could sell records without a hit single, so it wasn't shocking to her when *2112* started to do well. The music was good, but there was more to it than that. The band had struck a nerve, and record buyers responded.

"Did I think that it would make the fans happy who were feeling unheard, misunderstood, feeling like society was trying to crush them? Would it speak for them? Yeah, I believed it would," she said. "I believe it did, and I believe it still does."

At the time, the fans were primarily teenage boys, a cohort well known for feeling like someone is out to crush them. One didn't have to be under eighteen and possess a Y chromosome for the album to be relatable. Halper wanted to work in radio in the early 1970s when radio was a predominantly male industry with a "No chicks allowed" sign hanging on the clubhouse door. She fought her way in, but even then, she still faced opposition. She said she "absolutely could relate" to some of what's in *2112* as a result of that experience, and she wasn't surprised that other people could, too.

"Who hasn't been through a situation where they felt like society was trying to change them or where society was trying to force them into a box that they did not want to be in?" she asked. "The fans identified with Rush because who hasn't felt like society is telling you, 'You can't do this or you can't do that'? I thought the lyrics, the concept, would really speak to people in the Rush universe, and it might even bring in some new fans."

While *2112* had no clear hit single, it still gave the label more to work with than *Caress of Steel*, an album she characterized as "a little bit inaccessible." Sure, there was no "Love Will Keep Us Together" or "Have You Never Been Mellow?" in *2112*'s grooves, but it was a more confident and self-assured record than its predecessor, and it was listener-friendly without being dumbed down.

"I really believed the fans would relate to it," she said. "It told an important story, in addition to having a couple of other, shorter songs that I thought were really cool too. I thought the entire rock opera thing was just amazing. I thought it was creative. I thought the fans would really, really relate to it, and I thought it would resonate with them."

Lifeson said that once it became clear that the record was selling, the label adopted a hands-off approach. Mercury just let Rush be Rush.

"*2112* bought us our independence," Lifeson told NPR in 2016. "[Mercury] figured, 'Okay, they know what they're doing, and it works for them. As long as we're popping the cash register open, we're happy.'"

Geddy Lee plays an E major chord on one of his trademark double-neck Rickenbackers. Close inspection reveals that rather than one bass on top of another, this model had a bass at the top and a guitar at the bottom. Neat.

IN THROUGH THE OUT DOOR

3

AS AWKWARD AS THE *2112* ALBUM LISTENING PARTY at Mercury Records had been, it didn't change the band's plans for 1976. Rush still had a job to do, and that job was touring, night after night, city after city, just as they had been doing ceaselessly since the late summer of 1974.

After three dates in Ontario and one in Illinois, they got back to the grind of nightly touring on March 15, 1976. They began a run of four consecutive shows at Hollywood's fabled Starwood club, followed by an extensive North American tour lasting almost six months.

Given Mercury's reception to *2112*, the band may well have believed they would get the same puzzled response from concert audiences for the next half-year. They had already been through that demoralizing and expensive process on the *Caress of Steel* tour, and the idea of going through that all over again could not have been pleasant.

Ultimately, it was the only way forward, and whatever apprehensions they may have felt were not enough to outweigh their belief in the music and in the band. This thing was never going to work if they didn't go out there and conquer arenas one by one, so full speed ahead.

CLOCKWISE FROM RIGHT The cover of the tour program distributed to audiences during Rush's run of three shows at Toronto's Massey Hall in June 1976.

The *Fresno Mood* bootleg, which purports to be a recording of Rush performing at Selland Arena in Fresno, California, on November 28, 1976. This bootleg appears in multiple iterations with varying sound quality, so *caveat emptor*.

A view from the nosebleed seats depicts Rush as one would experience them from the back of the hall. With tickets going for less than $10, you can't really complain.

PREVIOUS Alex Lifeson, Neil Peart, and Geddy Lee wearing entirely too much makeup in a posed photo that makes them look like an exhibit at Madame Tussaud's wax museum.

On the *2112* tour, they shared stages with other 1970s hard rock acts such as Styx, Bad Company, and Thin Lizzy, whom they played with on April 17, 1976, in Pekin, Illinois. Like Rush, the Irish band were also promoting an album that would be their commercial breakthrough, *Jailbreak*. In 2005, Thin Lizzy guitarist Scott Gorham said that despite the differences in style and sound, Rush earned his band's respect the minute they started performing.

"We were street rock and they were on the progressive side," Gorham said. "The musicianship was incredible. 'All that musicality, all the intricacies, and all that power from just three guys . . . they really powered down on it. We respected the hell out of them."

A week later, Lee gave a telephone interview to the *Cleveland Plain Dealer* from a tour stop in Atlanta. He said that as far as he could tell, the changes to the band's music on *2112* seemed to be getting accepted by audiences.

"We're trying to put more emphasis on lyrics, on melody, more complete structures," he said. "We got some flak from some of our old fans, but we gained some new ones. I feel we are on a more sophisticated level."

He said the band had been touring the United States regularly with the intention of methodically building up a following there. It was a grind, but a strategic one; if they could establish themselves in the United States, other markets might follow suit.

He also said the band finally seemed to be breaking free of a comically exasperating situation in which U.S. audiences confused them with another Canadian band called Mahogany Rush. More importantly, there was no mention of the same sort of malaise that plagued the *Caress of Steel* tour.

The trio could tell from the stage that something was happening. They might never be an overnight sensation, but it was clear that their fortunes were starting to improve, and more people were starting to take notice of them.

"That was a very gradual thing," Lifeson told *Guitar World* in 2013. "We went from playing small venues to playing slightly less small venues. And we just continued on that rise."

It was a good thing that Rush had been touring heavily to build an audience because radio stations weren't going to lift a finger to help them then.

"We played 250 shows a year," he said. "We could see that we were becoming more popular, that people were becoming much more connected with our music. But we still had no airplay. So even as it was getting bigger, it felt like we were this kind of cultish band."

By the time they started a three-night engagement at Toronto's Massey Hall on June 11, 1976, few could deny that this group was catching on. In fact, that engagement was only supposed to be for two nights, but according to the 1982 book *Rush* by Brian Harrigan, the promoter was forced to add the third concert to meet demand.

On June 12, the date of the second Massey Hall performance, Peter Goddard wrote in the *Toronto Star* that the band's latest LP was gaining momentum in record shops after less than three months of release.

"*2112* has already sold 200,000 copies in the United States and nearly 35,000 copies in Canada," he said. He noted that 2,500 people had come to see the group play on opening night. They weren't curiosity-seekers either—these were committed fans who knew the songs and shouted along with every lyric. Furthermore, the Massey Hall run was being recorded for a live album.

Based on the recorded evidence, Rush's performances over those three nights were barnstormers. While they would develop a much more finessed approach to their performances later in their career, Rush circa June 1976 were a ferocious unit whose combined sound was metallic and furious.

"RUSH DO NOT TAKE THE STAGE SO MUCH AS ATTACK."

JIM SMITH in *Sound* magazine, 1976

"Rush do not take the stage so much as attack," Jim Smith wrote in Sound in 1976. "

"Alex Lifeson rips off a savage guitar riff. Geddy Lee drags out some heavy bass notes, and Neil Peart slams the drums mercilessly. The audience is roaring approval. . . . All of a sudden, Rush has become a musical force that must be taken seriously."

Smith interviewed Peart while the band was in Duluth, Minnesota, on May 23, 1976. They were sharing a bill with Blue Öyster Cult, but while the triumphant Massey Hall gigs were still a couple of weeks off, Peart was already saying the band had accomplished something. He indicated that it was due to numerous factors, many beyond the trio's control.

"Rush succeeded where other bands didn't for a lot of reasons, some of them outside the band," he said. "Part of our success had to do with good timing. A large part of it was due to good management."

The drummer did not forget to acknowledge that the group's quite active touring schedule had certainly moved the needle, too.

"The most important part, I suppose, was the fact that we worked very hard to get where we are now," he said. "We have been touring constantly since the first album was released, playing for thousands and thousands of people."

He acknowledged that the hit single route that had succeeded for other artists was likely not on the horizon for the Canadian trio. It just wasn't who they were.

"Either you concentrate all your energies into getting a hit single with massive airplay, or you get out and work a lot to get person-to-person contact with audiences," he said. "The latter approach seemed to be our only option. We're not inclined towards sounding like a top 40 band."

He added that in his opinion, airplay would only happen for Rush if they achieved a certain level of success first through touring. Then, and only then, might the band score a top 40 hit.

"We may get a hit record eventually, but it will only be because the radio stations have been forced," he said. "I think Aerosmith and Kiss are good examples of that: Radio stations didn't play those bands until their followings became so large that they couldn't be ignored."

Peart acknowledged that Rush faced certain hurdles as a three-piece unit when it came to expanding their sound. He said it was a positive situation because it was much easier for three people to find a creative equilibrium than seven

Aleksandar Živojinović, son of Nenad and Melanija, leads Neil Peart and Geddy Lee through an atmospheric musical passage.

people, or even four. It was better to stick with the configuration that appeared to be working.

"The three of us, for instance, are creatively balanced because we all write and we all arrange and we're all involved in the music right from the birth of an idea through to its recording," Peart said. "Right down to the very end, it is all split three ways, which is an even division that can't be found in larger bands. We have thought about adding a fourth member, but it would really tend to upset the chemistry and destroy our balance."

That July, *Maclean's* profiled Rush, another indication of the band's increasing profile. *Maclean's* is a mainstream Canadian publication and not an underground rock magazine, which meant the world beyond the heavy metal subculture was starting to pay attention.

For reasons best known to him, *Maclean's* writer Ken Waxman referred to the band as "little-known pretenders to punk rock's raunchy throne," a description that will never be even remotely accurate. Waxman quoted a fan he interviewed at a July 1976 concert in Texas, and she gave her reasons why she enjoyed the group's music so much.

"It's the energy level that really gets me off," she said. "They're bad."

The publication clarified that "bad" meant "good." It also said that 250,000 copies of *2112* had sold. This means that if the *Toronto Star* article's math was correct when citing 235,000 copies sold by July 12, 1976, then it had already sold another 15,000 copies when the *Maclean's* article was written. There had even been a spike in sales of the band's previous three albums, including the frequently disparaged *Caress of Steel*.

Describing the band members as "almost recklessly normal," Waxman said, "the three are about as far from the groupie-beset, drug-hazed image of rock stars as it's possible to imagine. They phone their parents after each concert and spend their time between performances in hotel rooms working on new music."

He also described the road regimen that Rush had withstood since 1974 as the key driver of their increasing success. Having a good album that people could connect to certainly went a long way, but they won their fans through touring.

"The band worked 50 weeks a year, often 14 days in a row, and kept to a punishing schedule that took it touring to every American state but four," he said.

On August 28, 1976, *Billboard*'s Starr Arning also made note of the band's arduous touring schedule of the previous two years.

"The Canadian band Rush has spent the last two years pouring all its energy and musical ingenuity into busting the competitive U.S. market open," Arning wrote. "No easy task, especially in the glutted area of hard rock. The fact that it's succeeding is a good indication that there's more to this band than just heavy metal guitar riffs."

On October 23, 1976, Graham Hicks wrote in the *Brandon (Manitoba) Sun* that the strategy of spending months at a time on American highways seemed to be bearing fruit. Rush had put in the time crisscrossing the Lower 48, and it seemed as though a barrier might be on the verge of breaking.

"The effort is paying off," Hicks said. "Their concept album, *2112*, was released in the United States earlier this year. It has sold 300,000 copies. Canadian groups are considered super-successful if they sell 100,000 copies of an album."

All the touring in the United States also had the effect of raising the group's profile in Canada. It seemed a little strange, but it was a fact—by touring the States over and over again, Rush ended up getting famous in the country where all three of them had been born and raised. In fact, when they sold out Massey Hall three nights in a row, they were the first Canadian band to do so.

Before all that, their own country had been somewhat indifferent to them. They may be the nation's favorite sons today, but as a young band on the rise, they weren't immediately embraced. They had to win Canadian hearts and minds by leaving the country and getting popular somewhere else.

"It was frustrating," Lee told Graham Hicks of the *Brandon (Manitoba) Sun* in 1976. "We were turned down by all the Canadian recording companies. We tried to hitch up on cross-Canada tours with major groups but were always being told Rush had no commercial potential. That was their favorite phrase."

The band smartly dealt with that situation by temporarily giving up on it. If they played the States enough to build a name for themselves, Canada would come around eventually.

"Since then it's been tour, tour, tour," Lee said. "We've played hundreds of American towns supporting whoever we could."

The strategy ultimately paid off. And there was no hit single.

"We don't seem to be a singles band," Lee said. "Mercury first signed us, thinking we'd have a string of hits like Bachman-Turner Overdrive. . . . But since *2112* was released, Mercury's given us a great deal of support."

He also said Rush's breakthrough was a boon for other Canadian groups. Artists from Montreal and Winnipeg could stop being regional sensations if they focused their touring on the States, but he felt that musicians from Toronto, in particular, would benefit the most from their strategy.

"We've shown musicians from Toronto could go to the U.S.A. and make it," he said. "Record companies are now aware of that. It's possible to be successful outside of your own backyard."

Throughout Rush's history, people frequently observed how amazing it was that these three unassuming dudes could create so much sound. Well, when you're the top musicians in your field, it only takes three people.

RUSH

WHAT A LONG STRANGE TRIP IT'S BEEN

4

RUSH WASTED NO TIME CAPITALIZING ON THE SUCCESS of their Massey Hall engagement. All three performances were recorded for their first live album, which was released to the public on September 29, 1976. It was a two-LP set called *All the World's a Stage*.

The final night of those concerts in Toronto was June 13, 1976. The release date of *All The World's a Stage* was just 108 days later. It's also worth noting that barely six months had elapsed since the release of *2112*. That's a mind-boggling amount of work for a single calendar year, which wasn't even over yet.

The live record was another effort shared by Terry Brown and the band. It was now their fifth time working together and their fifth time mixing at Toronto Sound. By now, the working relationship was in a groove; and while the sound quality on the finished record is a little raw by Rush standards, it was an accurate portrayal of the band at that point. They made a ferocious, uncompromising noise, one just technical enough to stand out from the multitudes.

"[*All the World's a Stage*] is an anthology of what we feel to be the high points of our concerts and recordings up to this time," the liner notes read. "It is not perfect, but it is faithful to us and to you. We have tried to strike a careful balance between perfection and authenticity."

The album started making the rounds among fans and critics. Notably, some members of the famously unreceptive press seemed to finally appreciate what Rush was trying to convey.

Peart told Anastasia Pantsios of *Circus* that the record company had been "hot" for a live Rush album. This may have been because of a recent spate of live double albums that had sold well and increased the profiles of numerous artists who had previously struggled to get to the next commercial plateau.

Alive! by KISS had been released in September 1975 and was the band's commercial breakthrough. It was followed early the next year by Peter Frampton's *Frampton Comes Alive!* and Bob Seger's *'Live' Bullet*. All three albums were wildly successful, and it's easy to see why. They were instant "greatest hits" packages, with versions of an artist's most popular songs presented with more energy, bombast, and crowd noise.

It's tempting to say that these albums were as popular as they were because of the onstage energy coming through the home stereo system; in many cases, though, live albums of the mid-1970s were not even a little bit live. Some classic, beloved 1970s live albums that shall remain nameless were masterpieces of post-production, with most of the sounds on the record overdubbed later in the recording studio. This even included applause in some cases.

All the World's a Stage was not such an album. Minus a couple of overdubs that the band have always confessed to, it was the real thing.

According to the 1982 book *Rush* by Brian Harrigan, Lee said there were a handful of vocal overdubs, a drum solo from one night edited into a performance from another, and guitar overdubs to "Working Man." Lifeson's overdubs became necessary in order to salvage a thundering and definitive take of the song that was sadly marred when he broke a string. Otherwise, *All the World's a Stage* was a live album that really was live, and the performances are so good that it would not be surprising if people who had never seen Rush perform decided to remedy that after hearing these fully unleashed live readings.

"We always felt there was something happening live that didn't come across on record," Peart said. "*All the World's a Stage* presents our material to people who may have heard or liked a couple of our songs but never got into all our albums."

Geoff Barton, writing in *Sounds*, gave the record exceptionally high marks. He had been a fan of the group since their debut, and he couldn't say enough good things about the two-LP set.

"Recorded over three nights at Toronto's Massey Hall, the LP literally seethes with mature heavy rock power, a live album to end all live albums," he said. "*All the World's a Stage* contains some of the best tracks from past band LPs, all performed immaculately, energetically and aggressively."

He ended the review by calling Rush "the best undiscovered band in Britain at the moment," a situation he likely hoped they would address by crossing the pond for a U.K. tour, sooner rather than later. That opportunity came in 1977. When the *2112* tour ended, Rush had exactly one week to decompress; then they turned right back around to start the *All the World's a Stage* tour.

That jaunt started on August 8, 1976, in Erie, Pennsylvania; and its last North American date was on May 22, 1977, in Port Huron, Michigan. They played damn near every night of the year during those nine months, and less than two weeks later, on June 1, 1977, they played their first U.K. date in Sheffield. They had never played outside North America before.

Barton was there on behalf of *Sounds*. It would be an understatement to call his review a "rave."

"Gods, throw all doubts to the wind, Rush are some band," he wrote. "The kids lap it up."

He also made the same observation many people have made about the band for decades.

CLOCKWISE FROM RIGHT As a great man once said, the waiting is the hardest part. Fans queue up outside of Chicago's Aragon Ballroom on May 20, 1977, during the *All the World's a Stage* tour.

The track listing on side one of *Everything Your Listeners Ever Wanted to Hear by Rush* . . . indicates radio-friendly selections, but radio remained unfriendly to Rush.

The absolutely hideous cover of the *Necromancer* bootleg, chronicling the band's June 1, 1977 concert in Sheffield, which journalist Geoff Barton reviewed in *Sounds*. "Gods, throw all doubts to the wind, Rush are some band," he wrote.

PREVIOUS Rush at Chicago's Aragon Ballroom on May 20, 1977, making the afternoon hours of waiting in line worth every minute for every fan who showed up.

While it's impossible to say what song Alex Lifeson, Neil Peart, and Geddy Lee are playing in this photo, we know it's not "Lessons" or "Tears" from *2112*, which were never performed live.

“LIVE, IT COMES TO LIFE, SO TO SPEAK, EVEN MORE SO THAN ON THE ALBUM.”

GEOFF BARTON in *Sound* magazine, 1976.

“For a three-man band Rush make a lot of noise,” he said. “Lifeson is everywhere, riffing, licking, soloing, plucking, and strumming all within the space of scant seconds. Lee, as well as playing a mean, dirty-sounding bass and singing, also contributes mini-Moog passages, playing the instrument’s floor-keyboard with his feet. Peart is a flashy, powerful drummer with an amazing amount of equipment at his disposal. It all amounts to, as I say, a lot of noise.”

Then it came time for the band to play the dystopian epic that was the centerpiece of their latest studio album. Despite the fact that during this period, the band would excise a couple of movements from “2112” when performing it live, Barton had no complaints about how the group pulled off this complex piece of music.

“Live, it comes to life, so to speak, even more so than on the album,” he said.

He added that he looked forward to seeing the band again a few days later in London. He urged those reading to see the band play the next chance they got.

“You’d be foolish to miss them, miss the shrill, piercing vocals of Geddy Lee, the virtuoso metal guitar playing of Alex Lifeson and the drum kit thunderings of Neil Peart,” he said. “Don’t know about the planets of the Solar Federation, but Rush have certainly assumed control of me.”

Of course, not everyone in the British press was as thrilled with the band as Barton. Andrew Harries of *Melody Maker* reviewed the band’s concert the next night in Manchester and was not impressed.

“Their quasi-political lyrics are an unusual feature, but it was difficult to hear them with Geddy Lee’s high-pitched shriek,” he wrote. “I found it dull, depressing, and dated.”

To his credit, Harries conceded that he was vastly outnumbered by the rabid Rush faithful. For those who had bought a ticket instead of seeing the concert for free on a press pass, it was revelatory.

"The place was packed and the audience reaction was extraordinary," he observed. "[Rush ignited] the two-and-a-half thousand denim-clad youngsters into fits of head-shaking frenzy and physical distortion."

It was a story that would repeat itself, over and over, for decades. The fans loved it and lapped up every drop, with no concern whatsoever about the critics and their highly contemptuous hot takes. If anything, whenever the critics slammed the group, it almost made being a Rush fan cooler.

The band's chilly relationship with more adversarial members of the press resulted in some amusingly petty moments. Jeffrey Morgan, aka "Machine Rock" of *Cheap Thrills*, who had said of *2112*, "I hate this one," expressed his indignation with the group's promotional apparatus when they failed to comp him a review copy of *All the World's a Stage*.

"Rush's promo company refuses to give me one, so screw them," he said.

He was reduced to reviewing snippets of the record that he'd heard on the radio and concluded that, based on those bits, the album was "a hot cooker." He signed off by saying, "Please, boys—lay off the mystic concepts for a while, huh?"

They did not.

What Morgan didn't get, but what Geoff Barton did, was that the mystic concepts were why fans showed up. Morgan had utterly missed the point in a fashion reminiscent of *The Simpsons'* Ned Flanders, when he said he enjoyed the movies of Woody Allen, "except for that nervous fella's always in 'em."

Barton termed Rush's music "sword and sorcery rock" in *Sounds*. He understood that the subjects Morgan believed the band should stay away from were *exactly* what fans were responding to with so much enthusiasm. They wanted sword and sorcery rock—and lots of it—and the critics were simply not in touch with the hard reality that their opinions were of no value to Rush fans.

"Once a member of the band, Peart's Tolkien-slanted fantastical visions were allowed to run riot," he said. "The effect was simply shattering."

He wrote that the fantasy topics and lyrical preoccupations were not new, citing "bands and artists that have, in the past, been much intrigued by the works of Tolkien, Moorcock, Howard, Burroughs, Eddison and others." He specifically cited Led Zeppelin, who had name-checked Mordor, Gollum, and Ringwraiths in multiple songs and also cited progressive rock artists such as Bo Hansson and Jon Anderson. But in his opinion, this Canadian band was the one that really got it right.

"Rush beat them all," he wrote, saying they had already mastered the prog-epic art form with the much-maligned *Caress of Steel*. "If 'The Fountain of Lamneth' had been an epic, then ['2112'] was a *pièce de résistance*."

The band was now unquestionably ascendant. Unfortunately, that still did nothing to win them even a minute of airplay. Mercury had done their best to get them on the radio, even creating a sampler LP for radio stations called *Everything Your Listeners Ever Wanted to Hear by Rush . . . But You Were Afraid to Play*.

The sampler featured the most radio-friendly tracks imaginable from *Fly by Night*, *Caress of Steel*, and *2112*, including acoustic feel-good material like "Making Memories" and "Lakeside Park." Those songs could have fit in seamlessly on pop radio, right alongside "Don't Go Breaking My Heart" by Elton John; so it made sense as an overture to radio stations who weren't familiar with the band.

It's the thought that counts. But ultimately, the sampler did not succeed in winning the band airplay. Nothing did.

"It seems that radio programmers don't believe we exist," Lee told Brian Harrigan in the book *Rush*. "No matter how many sellout shows

SECTOR ONE

SECTOR TWO

SECTOR THREE

Neil Peart, Geddy Lee, and Alex Lifeson during the *All the World's a Stage* tour.

we do, no matter how many albums we sell, they still don't seem to be interested."

Lee was not particularly preoccupied with that. By this point, he and his bandmates understood that their path to stardom was paved not with hit singles but protracted and interminable bus rides from one venue to the next. So, they kept touring.

"As long as we keep pulling in audiences and selling records, we believe that we're doing the right thing," he said. "Anyway, we've been on the road for so long now, I don't think we could imagine any other kind of lifestyle."

According to the liner notes in the *2112* 40th anniversary box set, the band played 140 shows between March 1976 and May 1977, including the U.K. dates. Their fortunes had risen considerably during that period, so any residual PTSD from the *Caress of Steel* tour had likely worn off.

Unfortunately, there would be new problems. They would return to England the following year for a sixteen-date tour, including a February 20, 1978, date at London's Hammersmith Odeon. Despite the fact that they were there promoting their 1977 *A Farewell to Kings* album, *2112* would act as the catalyst for a problem they never anticipated and which is still causing them headaches today.

THE NONCHALANT MUDSLINGING EXPRESS

5

IN THE JANUARY 5, 1978, edition of *Circus*, Max Thaler contributed an article called "Recognition Is Only Half the Fun," which had the subtitle, "Rush Audiences Grow Quickly as Critics Slowly Catch On." It described the situation that played out as the trio toured to promote *2112* and *All the World's a Stage*. Namely, the kids loved it, and the press didn't.

"Rush has never been appreciated by the critics, and none of their albums qualify as 'critic's choices,'" he said. "Their concerts are likewise either misconstrued, ignored, or often misjudged by most critics, despite public reactions to the contrary."

He had no idea how right he was. The band had already raised more than a few eyebrows by using Ayn Rand's writing as a lyrical inspiration. They talked her up in the press, they said they drew inspiration from her writing, and the *2112* liner notes bore a dedication to her "genius." While Lee and Lifeson had read her work, it primarily resonated with Peart; and he was always eager to talk about it.

ABOVE A year and a half after suffering the slings and arrows of the British press, Objectivist percussionist Neil Peart reads a book on his drum throne at Le Studio in Morin Heights, Quebec, during the October 1979 *Permanent Waves* sessions.

PREVIOUS Neil Peart at Chicago's Aragon Ballroom during the *All the World's a Stage* tour on May 20, 1977. T minus nine months before being called a fascist in the British press.

Sometimes, this led journalists to presume things about the band members. Brian Harrigan said in the 1982 book *Rush* that some members of the press perceived the musicians to be "raging right-wing capitalists," despite the fact that they had no songs about the private sector, much less raging ones.

In fairness, it must be noted that Peart didn't do himself any favors with some of the things he said in the press. When one says things in print publications as he did, proposing that "humanitarians are just the same as dictators," one may incur a little side-eye from journalists . . . or at least a few follow-up questions.

Still, when the band met with *New Music Express* writer Barry Miles, they had no idea what was about to hit them. What was supposed to be an interview with the band turned into an op-ed piece in which the journalist suggested that the band members were Nazis. It was only 1978, but he was already writing clickbait articles.

Barry Miles did not return requests for comment emailed to his official website. Therefore, just as we can only speculate about the creative impetus behind Vincent van Gogh's *Café Terrace at Night*, we must do the same for Miles' "Is Everybody Feelin' All RIGHT? (Geddit . . . ?)."

The article's subtitle was "The Gist of This Being That Heavy Metal Tourists RUSH Are All RIGHT-er Than Most, as MILES Discovers." In the first part, he talks mostly about the music; and it should be said that as far as that's concerned, he operates in good faith. One does not get the sense that he's going to listen to their music ever again, but his comments concerning the music itself are hard to find fault with, even if he felt it was no great shakes.

"I mean they're just a power-trio in the grand tradition of Cream, Nice, and Blue Cheer updated into the later 70s with voice echoes, foldback EQ, phasing on the drums, and a very sophisticated lighting system," he said. "Nothing to worry about."

Even when he makes fun of the band's stage show, its comic value vastly outweighs any malicious intent that may be attendant. Also, it's part of what the band

Alex Lifeson and Neil Peart perform in April 1977. In a 2012 interview with *High Times*, the guitarist recounted the experience of being called an Ayn Rand acolyte, describing it as surreal since he described her work as "a little too far out for me."

intended to present, so it's fair game if he wants to make fun of it. No harm, no foul.

"[Lifeson] and Geddy—who also plays bass and synthesizer—trot about on a white stage-sized Cossett carpet like excited poodles while a Cape Canaveral style lightshow keeps up the ol' visual excitement," he wrote.

So far, the piece was funny and alliterative. More importantly, all criticisms lobbed against the band were about the music or the performance, making them all very much above the belt.

He said that at a lot of other rock concerts he had attended, there seemed to be a degree of back-and-forth between the audience and the band. This Rush concert, meanwhile, appeared to be a one-way transaction, in which the band played and the audience watched them do it. Again, guilty as charged.

Then, after some chitchat about the Rolling Stones, the topic of conversation turned to Ayn Rand, and it all went off the rails.

"She's an obscure ultra-right-wing American cult writer of the late 30s and early 40s and, yes Rush follow her ideas," Miles wrote. "The epic '2112' is a re-write of her book *Anthem* and they also name their Canadian record label after the same book."

Once Rand came up, Peart and Miles started discussing the relative merits of Objectivism vis-à-vis socialism. It went about as well as those kinds

CLOCKWISE FROM RIGHT One year post-smear, Rush made their triumphant May 7, 1979, return to London's Hammersmith Odeon. Despite being characterized in the British press as crypto-Nazis, they were allowed back in the country anyway.

A *Circus* magazine article describes Rush's slow, methodical, and ultimately successful rise. "Rush audiences grow quickly as critics catch on slowly," the truthful subtitle said.

Rush outside the Birmingham, England, Holiday Inn on February 12, 1978. Ask about their convenient turndown service.

Recognition Is Only Half the Fun

Rush Audiences Grow Quickly as Critics Catch on Slowly

by Max Thaler

Rush are something of a classic North American rock band. They are young—in their early twenties—good looking, and dedicated to producing concert rock of the highest caliber, involving a sophisticated light show, extended arrangements, epic lyric writing, and the kind of musical attack that gets audiences rocking out of their seats."

"When they toured Britain recently they surprised a lot of people by selling out and getting a standing ovation at their gigs—not bad for a band virtually unknown here until recently."

Not bad for a band that had no critical respect for about four long years, despite ever-enlargening audiences and record-buying support. The kind, quoted words above, written by English *Melody Maker's* excellent correspondent Chris Welch, tell a long tale, one that Neil Peart, Geddy Lee and Alex Lifeson are tiring of. But they will ultimately have the last laugh.

Simply, Rush has never been appreciated by the critics, and none of their albums qualify as "critics' choices." Their concerts are likewise either misconstrued, ignored or often misjudged by most critics despite public reactions to the contrary. One *New Musical Express* headline ran as follows: "The Rush Phenomenon—This band has fans. Lots of them. They sold out the Free Trade Hall and surprised even the promoters." Obviously they didn't surprise the fans—enough of them, anyway, to sell the hall out.

Fortunately, stateside writers have been catching on, although the movement is still on the mostly local, groundswell level. Meaning, local newspapers, which are often closer to their readers' reactions than most of the "nationals," have been boosting Rush.

"Like a breath of fresh air in the misty haze of hard rock there stands a relatively new phenomenon with an ever-expanding following that calls itself Rush. For the edification of those ignorant few who think that Rush is just something you get when you smoke . . ." begins Mike Derevlany's July, 1977 review in *The Good Times*. Pete Bishop, in the *Pittsburgh Press*, following Rush's sixth successful gig in Pittsburgh, praises them for their best set ever.

Rush Whips Up a Perfect Frenzy. The Rush is Starting to Hit. A Caress of Steel. Rush: Hard Rock, Intelligent Lyrics. The headlines tell their stories; Rush is a crowd-pleaser, with or without the slow-to-react critical press.

Variety, that index of world entertainment, once summed it up: "It's an old story for rock groups in the 'heavy metal' or 'power rock' category. Traditionally, practitioners of this overly amplified sound, including Grand Funk Railroad, Aerosmith, Uriah Heep, Kiss, and others have met nothing more friendly than a stone wall when it comes to the powers who control airplay." (This was after Rush had sold out a Chicago auditorium nine days before the gig.)

But Neil Peart's message, "Be Honest," does a better job of explaining their direct line to their fans. "Our music has to be an honest statement of what we want to hear and what we want to play. Honesty is the keynote, the principle which we try to apply to everything we do—the music, the business, our personal relationships with each other." For young people, a rock band couldn't dedicate itself to better goals. And, luckily, Rush plays the kind of hard-driving rock that backs them up pretty well.

Paul Rambali, in *NME*, caught the critics/fans dichotomy cold: "Rush's ability in thir chosen field is unquestionable. No matter how overworked the basic idea may be, they attack it with enough ferocious zest and almost obsessive dedication that the results really did sound alive and, to the crowd at least, fresh." You bet!

Alex Lifeson, Neil Peart and Geddy Lee, backstage before a recent gig. Rush plays in excess of two hundred concerts a year, half in the US.

Kwasniewski/Star

CIRCUS MAGAZINE/33

of discussions always go, but in the exchanges between the two that Miles cited, one could still say the two men were just engaged in a feisty academic discussion that was all hypothetical.

At that point, Miles made statements about the band and their political leanings, all of which derived from his own fertile imagination, and a stubborn and enduring smear was born.

In fairness, Miles never used the word "Nazi," so there was nothing legally actionable about what he said. But he took egregious liberties with what Peart said, concluding that the band members were all fascists, an assumption he had spun entirely from whole cloth.

"So now I understood the freedom [Peart] was talking about," Miles wrote. "Freedom for employers and those with money to do what they like and freedom for the workers to quit (and starve) or not. Work makes free. Didn't I remember that idea from somewhere? 'Work Makes Free.' Oh yes—it was written over the main gateway to Auschwitz Concentration Camp."

After advancing the fiction that the members of Rush advocated Nazism, he accused them of preaching the philosophy from the concert stage to the suggestible youth in the audience. He also said the Red Star symbol used on the *2112* album cover was meant to symbolize socialism, then conceded that he was only "supposing" that was what it meant, never bothering to ask the musicians he was interviewing if that was the case.

"All the classic hallmarks of the right-wing are there," he said. "The use of a quasi-mystical symbol—the naked man confronting the red star of socialism (at least I suppose that's what it's supposed to be). It's all there."

Since he was sitting right there in person, he could have done a lot more than just suppose. He could have done his basic due diligence as a journalist and asked Peart if the Red Star was supposed to symbolize socialism. If the drummer had said yes, then everything Miles wrote in the rest of the article would have qualified as journalism. Instead, it was an exercise in character assassination that willfully misrepresented the band's point of view.

"Rush would like to return to the survival-of-the-fittest jungle law, where the fittest is of course the one with the most money," he concluded.

Rush author Brian Harrigan had introduced the band to Miles, whom he described as "a highly rated and highly respected writer by anyone's standards." As far as he knew, he had left Peart and Miles in a state of "spirited discussion," not thinking anything beyond that would transpire. When the magazine came out and he read the article, he was horrified.

"Miles had taken Rush to be little more than a bunch of crypto-fascists, and he was issuing stern warnings against the desirability of such a band playing in public," he said. "I was aghast."

Harrigan said he did not believe Miles had intentionally set out to try to smear the band. Indeed, he said the writer was calling it like he saw it, and maybe that's the truth of it. Still, Harrigan couldn't deny that whatever Miles intended, it sure looked like he'd had ulterior motives, whether that was true or not.

"There was no question of a deliberate axe job but all the same the results looked pretty damning in print," he said. At the same time, he said that on the plus side, every hard rock and heavy metal fan in the United Kingdom had now heard of the band, just as Geoff Barton had hoped.

The article was not well received by the band members, to say the least. Lifeson told *Rolling Stone* about the dustup in 2016, and he was still kind of mad about it.

"[Miles] set forth his point of view, and then Neil took the opposing view, as more of an exercise than anything," the guitarist said. "They ran it as this big exposé. It said that we were Nazis and we would leave our grandmothers starving in the street because we were so selfish and uncaring."

Miles' contention that the band espoused the "Work Makes Free" philosophy was easily the most hurtful thing in the article. It's not known whether Miles was aware Lee's parents had been imprisoned at Auschwitz, and one wants to give him the benefit of the doubt and conclude that he wouldn't have said it if he had known. But he saw no problem with calling the band members fans of tyranny based solely on what he supposed, and once he said the band advocated a "Work Makes Free" philosophy, it wasn't something he could just unsay.

"Geddy's parents came through the Holocaust, so he was very, very sensitive to that," Lifeson told *Guitar World* in 2013. "We were all very sensitive to that because of him."

For his part, Lifeson said he never considered himself anything but socially liberal, so being called a Nazi was kind of a weirdly novel sensation for him. He added that he had never really cared for Rand's writing all that much either, making the accusation that he was a devotee even weirder.

"I read one of [Rand's] books, but she was a little too far out for me," he told *High Times* in 2012.

Lee said he was distraught by Miles' article when he read it, for obvious reasons. He also told *PROG* that he had simply never had any authoritarian leanings in his entire life, and it was a bizarre and off-base thing to be accused of.

"The story in '2112' was very anti-authoritarian," he said. "It was all about freedom—creative freedom and individual freedom—so I was shocked when the *NME* called us neo-fascists. That's so far off the truth. It's crazy."

People in Rush's orbit were likewise grossed out by Miles' article. Terry Brown observed that he and many others thought the article had far exceeded any journalistic mandate and crossed a very clear line.

"I think it offended a lot of people," he said. "It offended me."

The experience was so unpleasant for Peart that he was loath to revisit the topic of Ayn Rand in subsequent years. Sean D. Naylor of *Feedback! Rock Interviews* broached the topic in a July 1983 interview, asking him if he thought the writer would have approved of rock music or the music of Rush, specifically. He gave a terse response.

"I've no idea, nor do I really care," he said.

Lifeson said the *NME* journalist was hardly the only person who completely misunderstood what the drummer got from Rand's books. Peart and Miles may have argued the economic implications of socialism versus Objectivism, but that was never the primary draw for the drummer. He saw Rand's writing as encouraging him to never compromise on his artistic vision. This was the inspiration behind "2112," despite Miles' insistence that it's secretly a twenty-minute song about how corporations are awesome and poor people deserve to die.

"['2112'] is a similar story to her stories of finding something that's beautiful and developing it, learning to share it, crafting it, and then being shut down by 'The Man,'" he said.

Music writer Rob Hughes said Peart's fascination with the author was understandable, considering that the drummer was young when he started reading her work. Her writing appealed to many adolescents and young adults as they've only just begun to grapple with their identities.

"At that age, you're trying on and burning through ideas faster than sneakers," he wrote. "When I listen to *2112* now, it reminds me of those restless years of figuring out how to negotiate the world and the people in it. Just as I can look back and see what a breakthrough *2112* was for Rush, I can remember being that naïve kid about to make a few breakthroughs himself."

It was ever thus. Donna Halper said even she was taken with Rand's books when she was young, at least for a little while.

Alex Lifeson, Geddy Lee, and Neil Peart want you to know that what you own is your own kingdom.

"In college, I liked Ayn Rand too," she said. "I don't know too many people in college who didn't."

She, too, said that many people got Rush's affinity for Ayn Rand wrong. They misunderstood what the band took from her work and why they responded to it.

"The interpretation that I've often seen lacks nuance," she said. "There's a big difference between 'being inspired by' and 'signing up for.'"

Harrigan said that eventually, after the *NME* article had been out for a while, the public did what it does best. It got bored, forgot about it, and moved on to the next outrage du jour. But he couldn't deny that while the affair had been painful for the band, the publicity did a lot to get its name out there in the United Kingdom, where they had been trying to establish themselves after conquering North America.

"In a curious way, I think Miles' article helped to establish the band somehow," he said.

As for Miles, who feared that Rand's influence on Rush would midwife the Fourth Reich into existence, he can take some comfort in the fact that Objectivism never really caught on. In fact, according to the Ayn Rand Institute, Ayn Rand collected Social Security, so even Ayn Rand was too much for Ayn Rand.

GEDDY
ALEX
NEIL
FRAGILE

TWENTY-FIRST CENTURY 2112

ON DECEMBER 16, 2016, a 40th Anniversary Edition of *2112* was released. It features the original 1976 album, and, according to the band's official website, it used the "much-acclaimed 2015 hologram vinyl edition" made at Abbey Road Studios. It was the first appearance of that specific mastering on compact disc.

The album is accompanied by a second disc, containing "rare, live, and previously unreleased material." It includes three live tracks by the band and a one-minute radio spot from 1976 that accurately describes the record as "a concept of life in the future conceived and performed by Rush." The package also contains an entirely useless exercise called "Solar Federation," which is eighteen seconds long and consists of Peart's isolated vocal at the end of "2112" saying, "Attention all planets of the Solar Federation. . . ." If you ever wondered what the end of "2112" sounds like with the sound of the band removed, this is your chance.

The set also includes five songs from *2112* recorded by other artists, such as Dave Grohl, Taylor Hawkins, Steven Wilson, and Alice in Chains. Jacob Moon's cover of "Something for Nothing" is a high point. He intelligently takes an entirely different approach to the song's arrangement and does not attempt to be faithful to the original in any way. This unique take works because his reframing works.

Alice in Chains' version of "Tears" gets a reworking reminiscent of "Down in the Hole" from their classic *Dirt* album. They've chosen to sound like themselves here and not try to emulate the original, which was the smart move.

These covers work best when the artist reinvents them through their own sensibility. It's all good stuff, but ultimately, only Rush can really play Rush. In that sense, they were like the Rolling Stones, the Beatles, and Led Zeppelin. Only they could sound like themselves, no matter how faithful the tribute, making the live recordings included in the set welcome alongside the covers by outside artists.

There are three live recordings included in this package. One is "The Twilight Zone" from 1977, which the liner notes describe as "Contraband." What they mean to say is that the sound quality is absolutely atrocious.

The recording is included because the song was only performed live twice in the band's history. When the tape hiss briefly recedes enough for the performance to poke through, it's up to the usual Rush standard. But the trebly swishing inherent in the recording is very distracting, making the track only of interest to the most hardcore completist. It's there for posterity, and that's about it.

What remains of the live stuff are two recordings from Massey Hall that weren't included on *All the World's a Stage*. Per the set's liner notes, the version of "2112" here is taken from the first night on June 11, 1976. Terry Brown said, "It sounds deadly," and he wasn't kidding. If the powers that be wanted to release a box set of all three complete concerts from the Massey Hall 1976 run, nobody would complain.

RIGHT 1970s-era Alex Lifeson, Neil Peart, and Geddy Lee watch over their April 18, 2013, counterparts' performance at the Rock and Roll Hall of Fame Induction Ceremony in Los Angeles.

PREVIOUS Over and out. Directors' chairs bearing the band members' names in the Civic Auditorium dressing room on September 26, 1977, Bakersfield, California.

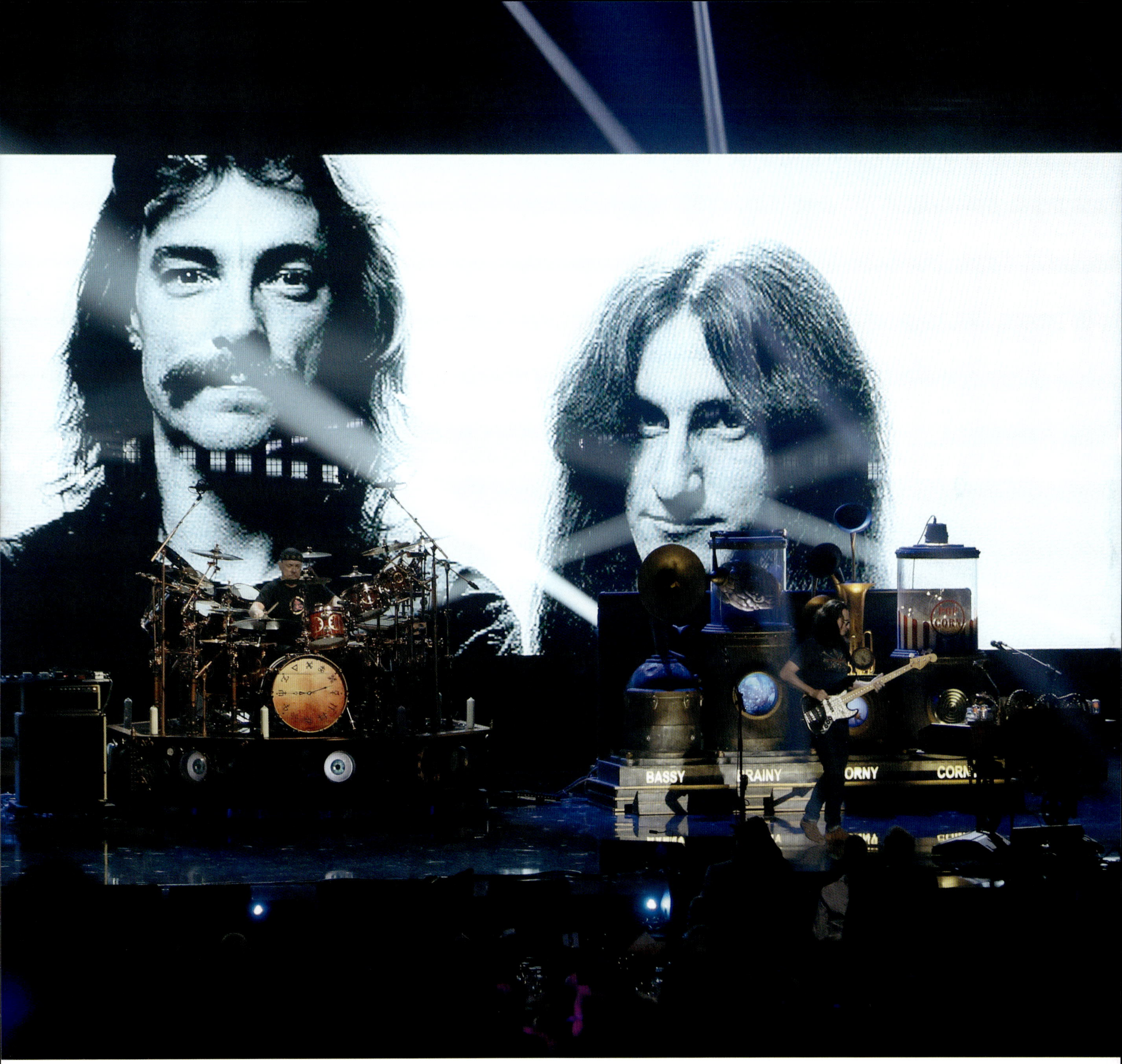
BASSY

CLOCKWISE FROM LEFT Rush bolsters their image as the most Canadian band in the world by posing with two Mounties at the 2011 JUNO Awards in Toronto.

Geddy Lee, Neil Peart, and Alex Lifeson at their RockWalk induction at Guitar Center in Los Angeles on November 20, 2012, a mere hundred years before the events depicted on their fourth LP.

The *Capitol Punishment* bootleg, which purports to be Rush's April 17, 1977, concert at George Washington University's Lisner Auditorium in Washington, D.C. As is the case with other bootlegs mentioned in this book, the dates and venues are *probably* right. Having said that, no promises.

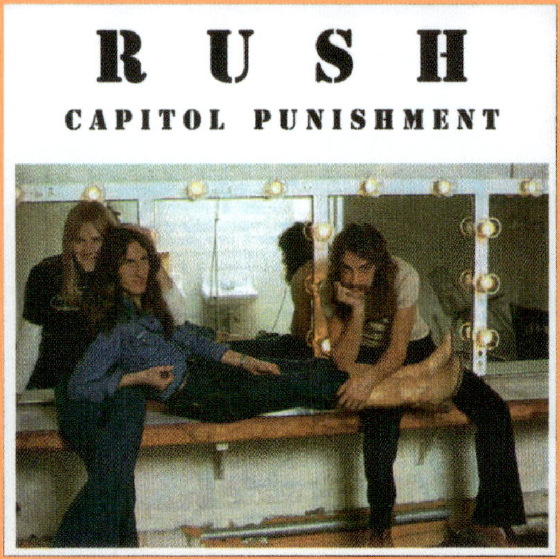

The performance omits the "Discovery" and "Oracle: The Dream" movements. This was standard operating procedure during every performance of "2112" during this era. As the years passed, they continued omitting sections, ultimately whittling the suite down to "Overture" and "The Temples of Syrinx." During the 1996 tour for *Test for Echo*, however, the band played all seven movements of the song in their entirety, to great effect.

The other outtake from the Massey Hall concerts is "Something for Nothing." While it's not drastically different from the studio version or the one that made it onto *All the World's a Stage*, it's still a high-energy reading of the song; and Peart produces explosive drum fills for days. We are richer as a species for having this recording available.

The box also includes a DVD featuring interviews with Lifeson and Terry Brown and a six-song performance from the Capitol Theatre in Passaic, New Jersey, on December 10, 1976. The concert is excellent, but the performances of "Bastille Day," "Anthem," and "2112" are particularly savage.

If this performance is anything to go by, Rush circa 1976 was a live act that took no prisoners and played at the highest level every night. It's easy to see how Rush could have won over some uninitiated person who was just there to drink a few beers and listen to Foghat.

One viewing of this concert is all it takes to understand how Rush connected with thousands of listeners by going on the road. They took the music directly to the people, night after night, and won every fan in real time.

In the decades since *2112* was released, the band members have been asked if they have any regrets about how the record turned out. With the benefit of hindsight, had any of them concluded that they had erred in any of the choices that made the record what it is today?

While he rued nothing, Lifeson told *Rolling Stone* in 2016 that at least one aspect of the 1976 album could have aged better—the band's fashion sense. *2112* has a striking cover with a distinct visual sense, but he did not fondly remember being photographed for it. He described the photo session as "very awkward" for the whole band, none of whom particularly enjoyed that kind of stuff.

"We took that photo with a fashion photographer," he said. "I think the photographer made the suggestion to dress up all in white with a wind machine."

Otherwise, the guitarist had no issues with the cover decades later. In fact, he said that it never surprised him that Hugh Syme's "Starman" art has held up all these years.

"I thought it was really powerful when Hugh showed it to us," he said. "It just seemed so iconic that we knew then that this would last for a long time."

2112 has proven to be the record where a lot of untried methods converged with timeless results. That goes for the songs, the performances, the sound quality, and the story. Lifeson's gripes with the band photos aside, everything about *2112* was on point.

"'2112' took you somewhere," wrote journalist Rob Hughes. "You can see it all playing out in your mind's eye."

One of the things that's always kept the "2112" story compelling is the vague ending, which can be interpreted as either the end of the world or the destruction of the Death Star. Hughes offered his own interpretation.

"I always interpreted the '2112' suite's ending as destruction preceding renewal," he said. "The voice that announces, 'We have assumed control,' comes from neither the priests nor the hero. It's the voice of hope."

Really, how many rock albums, classic or otherwise, have inspired decades of debate among

Disciples of 2112

Musicians have never been shy about expressing their admiration for Rush. The number of people who play musical instruments and cite them as a primary influence is beyond number, and it's easy to see why. Those guys could play like few others, and it's not hard to imagine young, impressionable musicians looking to Lee-Lifeson-Peart as an example and wanting to reach their same virtuoso level.

As a result, the musicians they've inspired have tended to be a cut above the rest in their own right; and many of them have said the album that did it for them was *2112*. In 2016, Lifeson told *Rolling Stone* that inspiring new generations of artists with this record had been a privilege for him.

"I think the influence that it had on a lot of listeners, just judging from the comments I read in the mail and even comments from other bands that have been influenced by us, that's really a signature record for all of them," he said. "That's a wonderful thing. If you're going to leave something as your legacy, having something that is so influential on other people that it has improved their lives or just made them more understanding of something, I think that is the ultimate."

Drummer Chad Smith of Red Hot Chili Peppers said in the 2016 short documentary *A Salute to Kings* that as a high school student in Michigan in the 1970s, the *2112* album played a central role in his decision to become a full-time musician. He could already play, and he performed in a band with some older classmates, but hearing *2112* turned his hobby into the thing he wanted to do for the rest of his life.

"The eight-track that was the soundtrack to my sophomore year in high school was *2112*," he said, recalling sitting in a car with his bandmates every morning when he was supposed to be in class. "It would be freezing cold in Detroit, and the windows would be down, and we would smoke a lot of weed and listen to *2112* over and over and over. I never really ever made it out of the parking lot into school."

Peart became his idol in short order. After seeing the group perform at Joe Louis Arena, he said he started setting up his drum kit to be identical to that of the man he looked up to.

"I had little roto toms, and the splash symbols, and the cowbells, and I would play in my basement in Detroit, put on the headphones and play to that record," he said. "It changed my life."

Taylor Hawkins of Foo Fighters was also enormously influenced by the 1976 record. It was the first Rush record he had ever heard, and it immediately stuck.

"The overture grabbed me," he said. "I liked the fact that it was really hard rock. I loved Yes and Genesis when I was 10 or 12, but most of those prog bands were not really heavy. Not like *2112*, which mixed heavy metal with technical stuff. . . . It was as hard as Sabbath or Zeppelin, but the technicality was on a whole other level."

Bjorn Gelotte and Peter Iwers of the Swedish death metal band In Flames are also big fans. In fact, they're such big fans that they opened a restaurant in the Swedish city of Gothenburg and named it 2112.

The menu contains several different beef burgers with musical themes, such as the "It's Not Unusual," the "Smoke on the Water," and, of course, the "In Flames." But if you're going to fly to Sweden to go to a restaurant called 2112, you might as well go all in and get the "2112 Famous Burger," with white truffle mayonnaise, aged cheddar, lettuce, tomato, and onion. Be sure to specify single or double, although it should be noted that the double is a mere 50 Swedish krona more, so why not treat yourself?

In 2013, Lee said that while he had not visited the restaurant, he had heard of its existence and was moved by the gesture.

"It's a huge compliment when someone thinks so much of your music that they are inspired to name a restaurant after you," he said.

Barney Greenway of Napalm Death said he was also a big fan. If *2112* seems an unlikely inspiration for the death metal musicians of In Flames, consider that Napalm Death are primarily known for their extreme brevity, as typified by their 1989 song "You Suffer." That particular ditty clocks in at one second long, so that band is nothing if not terse. Still, he told *PROG* in 2014 that his favorite Rush song was all twenty minutes and thirty-three seconds of the title suite.

"I'd go for '2112,' despite its length," he said. "The track's so catchy and has some very heavy moments. There's a riff in there that's really powerful."

While there's nothing new about musicians worshipping at the altar of Lee-Lifeson-Peart, *2112* is not the album that usually gets mentioned the most. That distinction belongs to 1981's *Moving Pictures*, which remains the band's most popular album. But *2112* has plenty of its own boosters in the hard rock and heavy metal world, and Lifeson said that he thought its theme is what grabbed them. They took its message and used it as a rallying cry for their own musical efforts, especially if they faced opposition from their label.

"They'll say, 'We're big Rush fans, because they did it on their own, they did it their own way, and that told me that I could do the same thing,'" the guitarist said in 2016. "'If I stick with it, persevere, I can do things the way I want them to be.'"

CLOCKWISE FROM TOP Dave Grohl and Taylor Hawkins of Foo Fighters induct Rush into the Rock and Roll Hall of Fame on April 18, 2013. It is worth firing up YouTube to watch *Rolling Stone*'s Jann Wenner struggle to be heard over the screaming of rabid fans as he grudgingly announces them.

Mike Portnoy of Dream Theater in Tokyo on November 18, 1992. Portnoy has repeatedly cited Neil Peart as one of his biggest influences as a drummer, which is readily apparent to anyone who listens to him play.

Chad Smith of Red Hot Chili Peppers in 1992. He credited a combination of cannabis, truancy, and an 8-track tape of *2112* for his decision to become a full-time musician.

listeners about what the ending means? They're out there, of course. Pink Floyd's *The Wall* comes to mind, and the Who did it twice, with *Tommy* and *Quadrophenia*. But otherwise, the list of rock concept albums with an ending open to interpretation is not a long one.

2112 is an unmatched hard rock concept album in another respect—its detailed world-building. The level of world-building and story development in "2112" come through so loud and clear that people began adapting it for different media, such as video games.

"It's official," *Rolling Stone* announced. "*Guitar Hero: Warriors of Rock* has the most epically prog-rock sequence of any music video game yet. Rush have teamed with Activision for the fall release, which features a story-based Quest Mode."

Lifeson thought the game could serve a dual purpose. While quest progression and other such features were one thing, he was primarily interested in how the game could help promote music among young listeners.

"I think it's a great way to introduce people of all ages to music of various styles by all kinds of different bands while providing a launching pad for kids who want to get into playing music," he said.

Still, even with state-of-the-art technology, nobody is going to care about the game if the story sucks; and in addition to the music, the reason "2112" has held up is the story. On that score, Greg Bouchard of *Vice* said it was no mystery why the suite's lyrics have connected with listeners for decades.

"There comes a time in every teen's life when, through a cocktail of hormones, angst, and Ayn

Many of Alex Lifeson's guitars were on display at Julien's Auctions on April 11, 2022, including a 1970 Les Paul and 1976 J-55 acoustic, both used in the recording of *2112*.

Rand, they envision themselves as the protagonist in a dystopian novel," he said. "'2112' . . . captures that moment in all its glory and ugliness. It's a classic free-thinking-loner-against-society tale, like *1984* or *The Matrix*, but with a monsoon of riffage and guitar solo wizardry."

He gave a one-paragraph summary of the plot. After describing the Temples of Syrinx, ancient instruments, and the autocratic suppression of creativity, he engaged in a little editorializing.

"This is just about the nerdiest shit ever, but with Rush, that's the charm," he wrote. "At some point growing up, everyone lived out a similar story in their daydreams, whether 'The Priests' were their parents or their school principal or a small town that didn't get them. With nothing else to do and nowhere to go, loneliness turns to escapism, escapism turns to fantasy, and fantasy turns to Rush."

Bouchard also mentioned the most obvious reason we're still discussing *2112* today: The music is timeless and immediate, no matter how many musical fads come and go.

"'A Passage to Bangkok' boasts one of the sickest rock riffs in the band's catalogue, with enough power and blues grit to make Black Sabbath jealous, while 'Lessons' is one of the most overlooked pop gems from their early career," he said. "When you consider how well it catered both to rock nerds and rock jocks, it's a lot less surprising that *2112* was Rush's first major success."

What about the people who made it? Do they know why people still listen to *2112* decades after it was made?

In 2014, Peart told *CBC Music* that the album was the product of sincere emotion, which came through when they recorded it. Peart said Mercury's suggestion that they write hit singles was "just like poison" to him, and the resulting rage and frustration came through the vinyl. It sounded like these guys really meant what they were saying, even if you missed a couple of plot points.

Geddy Lee at a speaking event for his 2023 memoir, *My Effin' Life*, in Quebec City on July 13, 2024. Attentive superfans will note his Le Studio T-shirt, commemorating the facility where they made their last three records with co-producer Terry Brown.

JOHNSON
51

"We were so angry at that time," he said. "We fought back. The tale happens to be about the individual against oppression, and that was us, it's how we felt. And it worked, it was our commercial breakthrough with a 20-minute song on one side. It spoke."

Lee co-signed on Peart's version of events in *PROG*. With *2112*, the band had given it everything they had, and listeners could tell. They responded.

"My sense is that there was a lot of passion in that record, there was a lot of ferocity in that record, and it cut through," he said. "It had a sound that was really pretty different from anything else going on at that time . . . it reached people."

Lifeson said that over the years, he's gone back and listened to the record for his own enjoyment, something not every musician likes to do. Fellow Canadian musician Neil Young, for example, told *MOJO* in 1995 that he never listens to his own records once he's made them.

"I spend so much time making them that when it's over, I just never want to listen to them again," he said. "I just send them out into the world like an evil father."

Lifeson, meanwhile, has thrown on *2112* on several occasions and is always rewarded by the experience.

"When I go back and listen to the original record, I feel really proud of it," he said. "I can still remember how I felt at the time we were making it, and how important it seemed, and how satisfied we all were when it came together. We felt we played really well on it, and the recording experience was fantastic. We were such a real team holed up in that studio of Terry's."

Brown remembered the *2112* sessions fondly as well. In fact, he characterized his entire working relationship with Rush in positive terms. He and the band would go on to make five more studio albums together after *2112*, including the most successful record of their career, 1981's *Moving Pictures*. The band and Terry Brown parted ways professionally in 1983, but when Rush started releasing retrospective box sets to commemorate the 40th anniversaries of their albums, those boxes contained live content from the period, mixed by Brown.

Despite the passage of decades, the band and the co-producer still have a fruitful relationship. He said that after *2112*, there might have been a handful of moments in which he and the band didn't quite see eye to eye, though it was never enough of a problem to negatively color his memories of their association. And decades later, he still remembered making the band's breakthrough 1976 album as an especially enjoyable experience of which he loved being a part.

"We always had so much fun making records," he said. "But back in the days of *2112*, we were young and enthusiastic, we were excited about the way it sounded, the material, and where it was going. It seemed so easy, to be honest with you. I don't remember it being a difficult process at all. It was a lot of fun to make. We just had a blast making that record."

Arizona Diamondbacks Hall of Fame pitcher and Rush superfan Randy Johnson is presented a Neil Peart signature drum kit during his jersey retirement ceremony on August 8, 2015.

ACKNOWLEDGMENTS

I AM DEEPLY GRATEFUL to the following people, who worked alongside Rush and let me interview them:

- Terry Brown, co-producer, *2112*
- Donna L. Halper, Ph.D., music historian
- Hugh Syme, album cover designer, *2112*

Special thanks to Dr. R. Douglas Helvering, composer and host of the *Daily Doug* YouTube channel, for explaining what an overture is, among other things. Thank you to musician Angie Scarpa for inspiring me to dig deeper into the concept of Rush as a punk rock band. Additional thanks to Donna L. Halper, Ph.D., for keeping copies of every press clipping the band ever got during the print journalism era.

I would like to express additional gratitude to Guy Charbonneau, Le Mobile recording engineer. Thank you for helping me contact Terry Brown and telling him I'm "not an asshole." In this day and age, that counts for a lot.

Thank you to my parents, Albert and Joanna Bukszpan; my sister, Claudia Rutherford; and my mother-in-law, Valborg Linn, for being in my corner and supporting me as I build my vast literary empire.

From the good people at Quarto-Motorbooks, thank you to Dennis Pernu and Jordan Wiklund for giving me the chance to write an entire book about an album I love. Thanks also to photo researcher Stuart Pease, who did a phenomenal job helping me illustrate this book. I never thought I would get the chance to write about this band once, to say nothing of doing it twice. An embarrassment of riches!

Thanks to my son, Roman, for being the best son on earth and giving the best high school graduation speech ever. Finally, thank you to my wife, Asia, the love of my life, and the woman who keeps loving me as I am. I love you and Roman more than anything in the world. I know I say it in every book, but it's the truth. Everything I accomplish means a lot more to me because you two are in my life when it happens.

Thank you to the band's official website, rush.com, for keeping the discography and tour information updated and available. Recognition is also due to the tireless efforts of these fan sites, which have kept comprehensive and thorough records of everything Rush for years. Researching this book would have been much more difficult without them:

- 2112.net
- cygnus-x1.net
- rushisaband.com

Finally, thank you to Geddy Lee, Alex Lifeson, Neil Peart, and Terry Brown for making this timeless, relevant record. The message resonates, the music is top-notch, and people will still listen to it long after we're all gone.

BIBLIOGRAPHY

BOOKS

Berti, Jim, and Durrell Bowman, eds. *Rush and Philosophy: Heart and Mind United*. Open Court, 2011.

Harrigan, Brian. *Rush*. Omnibus Press, 1982.

Lee, Geddy. *My Effin' Life: From Holocaust Roots to Rock and Roll Stardom*. Harper, 2023.

Peart, Neil. *Traveling Music: The Soundtrack to My Life and Times*. ECW Press, 2004.

Price, Carol Selby, and Reverend Robert M. Price, Ph.D. *Mystic Rhythms: The Philosophical Vision of Rush*. Borgo Press, 1999.

Stanyard, Stewart T. *Dimensions behind the Twilight Zone*. ECW Press, 2007.

ARTICLES

Arning, Starr. "Rush Rushes into U.S. Prominence." *Billboard*, August 28, 1976.

Barker, Gerry. "Futuristic Concept Album Proves Above Average." *Fort Worth Star-Telegram*, May 21, 1976.

Barth, Chris. "Rush on Bringing *2112* to 'Guitar Hero.'" *Rolling Stone*, July 20, 2010.

Barton, Geoff. "*All the World's a Stage* Review." *Sounds*, November 1976.

Barton, Geoff. "Poor Man's Zeppelin? Or Underrated Scions of Sword and Sorcery Rock?" *Sounds*, February 5, 1977.

Barton, Geoff. "We Have Assumed Control." *Sounds*, June 11, 1977.

Begrand, Adrien. "All the Gifts of Life: 40 Years of Rush's '2112.'" npr.org, April 30, 2016.

Bienenstock, David. "Alex Lifeson: The High Times Interview." *High Times*, June 2012.

Bienstock, Richard. "Big Time Rush." *Guitar World*, April 2013.

Blakeslee, David. "A Journey through the Eclipse Series: Allan King's Come on Children." criterioncast.com, December 9, 2012.

Bouchard, Greg. "Retrospective Reviews: Rush's '2112.'" *Vice*, August 25, 2014.

Daly, Skip. "Ian Grandy Interview: Rush's First Roadie." guitarinternational.com, September 16, 2009.

"Dine with Rush Theme for Polydor's Radio Promotion." *RPM Weekly*, March 6, 1976.

Dome, Malcolm. "'They Had the Uncanny Ability to Make Odd Meter into a Catchy, Radio-Friendly Experience': Hawkind, Dream Theater, Styx, Def Leppard, Manic Street Preachers, Napalm Death Members and Others Name Their Favourite Rush Songs." *PROG*, October 11, 2024.

Elliott, Paul. "All the World's a Stage." *Q Classic*, July 2005.

Elliott, Paul. "The History of Rush by Geddy Lee & Alex Lifeson: From Rebirth to Retirement." *Classic Rock*, August 7, 2016.

Elliott, Paul. "The History of Rush by Geddy Lee & Alex Lifeson: The Early Years." *Classic Rock*, February 3, 2016.

Elliott, Paul. "Men at Work." *PROG*, April 2013.

Elliott, Paul. "Rush Make 2112, 1976." *MOJO*, March 2016.

Ghate, Onkar. "The Myth about Ayn Rand and Social Security." Ayn Rand Institute, June 19, 2014.

Goddard, Peter. "Rock Trio Is a Threat to Old Massey Hall." *Toronto Star*, June 12, 1976.

Golsen, Tyler. "The Rush Song Inspired by a Classic TV Show." *Far Out*, January 19, 2022.

Grow, Kory. "Rush's Alex Lifeson on 40 Years of 2112: 'It Was Our Protest Album.'" *Rolling Stone*, March 29, 2016.

Hiatt, Brian. "From Rush with Love.'" *Rolling Stone*, June 16, 2015.

Hicks, Graham. "Rush Is Coming to Town." *Brandon (Manitoba) Sun*, October 16, 1976.

Hicks, Graham. "Rush Takes American Path to Find Stardom in Rock," *Brandon (Manitoba) Sun*, October 23, 1976.

"How Rush Made Fly by Night, by producer Terry Brown." *Classic Rock*, March 8, 2021.

Johnson, Howard. "'I Was Trying to Get Them Laid'—What Happened When Rush Toured with Kiss." *Classic Rock*, January 5, 2022.

Jovanović, Marko. "Geddy Lee Shares His Parents' Holocaust Story, How They Met in Work Camp & How They Survived Auschwitz." ultimate-guitar.com, February 3, 2019.

Kent, Nick. "I Build Something Up, I Tear It Right Down: Neil Young at 50." *MOJO*, December 1995.

Lalaina, Joe. "60 Minutes: Alex Lifeson of Rush." *Guitar World*, July 2006.

Lee, Geddy, Alex Lifeson, and Neil Peart. "The Story of '2112.'" *Live at Massey Hall Official Program*, June 11–13, 1976.

Machine Rock. "A Solid Gold Rush." *Cheap Thrills*, January 1977.

Marshall, Wolf. "Alex Lifeson: The Making of a Guitar Legend." *Guitar One*, September/October 1996.

Milano, Brett. "'2112': Rush's Landmark Album Explained." udiscovermusic.com, March 1, 2025.

Miles, Barry. "Is Everybody Feelin' All RIGHT? (Geddit . . . ?)." *New Music Express*, March 4, 1978.

Morgan, Jeffrey. "From Brainwaves to Tidal Waves: The Story behind Rush's Album Covers." *Creem*, Spring 1983.

"Mystic Rhythms: Rush's Neil Peart on the First Rock Drummer." npr.org, January 6, 2015.

Naylor, Sean D. "Neil Peart of Rus." *Feedback! Rock Interviews*, July 1983.

"Neil Peart on Rockline for Roll the Bones." *Rockline*, December 2, 1991.

Nooger, Dan. "Rush Goes into Future Shock: 'Music Will Not Exist in 2112.'" *Circus*, April 27, 1976.

Noth, Pierre-René. "Sounds of the Times." *Milwaukee Journal*, March 24, 1976.

Pantsios, Anastasia. "Rush Release: Canada's Power Trio Is Switched on Live." *Circus*, November 25, 1976.

Peart, Neil. "'Neil Peart Speaks with Zildjian . . . 'Who Were Some of Your Early Drum Influences?'" zildjian.com, January 2003.

Rauf, Raziq. "Mechanical Animals." *PROG*, April 2013.

"Rush: *2112*." *Shreveport (LA) Times*, April 11, 1976.

"Rush Dedicates Newest Album to Rod Serling." *St. Catharines Standard*, October 10, 1975.

"Rush Puts More Stress on Lyrics." *Cleveland Plain Dealer*, April 23, 1976.

"Rush's Geddy Lee: 'Punk Bands Made Us Seem Like Beethoven by Comparison.'" *The Guardian*, November 16, 2023.

"Rush's Longtime Producer Terry Brown Pays Tribute to Neil Peart: 'I Have So Many Fond Memories.'" blabbermouth.net, January 11, 2020.

Sharma, Amit. "Geddy Lee Talks Rush's *2112* Track-by-Track." musicradar.com, February 15, 2016.

Shteamer, Hank. "Rush's Geddy Lee: My 10 Favorite Bassists." *Rolling Stone*, July 2, 2020.

Smith, Jim. "A Headlong Rush to Stardom." *Sound*, July 1976.

Spencer, Hugh. "Social Justice from the Twilight Zone: Rod Serling as Human Rights Activist." *Dialogue: The Interdisciplinary Journal of Popular Culture and Pedagogy* 5, no. 1 (2018):1–13.

Swann, Elizabeth. "'We Went from Playing High School Dances Once or Twice a Month to Playing Six Nights a Week.' Alex Lifeson Tells How One Change Helped Rush's Career Take Flight." *Guitar Player*, April 17, 2025.

Terry, Josh. "Cloud Nothings Listens to Rush's '2112' for the First Time." *Vice*, December 27, 2018.

Thaler, Max. "Recognition Is Only Half the Fun: Rush Audiences Grow Quickly as Critics Slowly Catch On." *Circus*, January 5, 1978.

Waxman, Ken. "All Hail the Heirs Apparent!" *Maclean's*, July 1976.

"*2112* Press Kit." *Mercury Records*, February 23, 1976.

"*2112*, Rush." *Saskatoon (Sask.) Star-Phoenix*, April 30, 1976.

"*2112*—Rush." *Windsor (Ontario) Star*, April 24, 1976.

"*2112* by Rush." *Meriden (CT) Record & Journal*, March 27, 1976.

RECORDS

Bowman, Rob. "Liner Notes." *2112* 40th Anniversary Box Set, Mercury Records, 2016.

Peart, Neil. "Liner Notes." *2112*, Mercury Records, 1976.

WEBSITES

academia.edu
amazon.com
ari.aynrand.org
blabbermouth.net
cygnus-x1.net
faroutmagazine.co.uk
howstuffworks.com
hyperrust.org
imdb.com
journaldialogue.org
loudersound.com
npr.org
riaa.org
rollingstone.com
rushisaband.com
rushvault.com
terrybrown.net
udiscovermusic.com
vice.com
22.n11et

PHOTO CREDITS

Bob Alford: 9l, 106, 125, 132, 135, 138l, 141, 148.

Alamy: Peregrine: 62; Pictorial Press: 57;
Retrorocket: 119b; Some Tattered Old Things: 116.

Associated Press: *The Canadian Press*: 164t; FR170363 AP: 170; Invision: 163, 164br, 167tr; SIPAPRE: 168, 169.

Cygnus-x1.net: 99bl, 113, 156br.

Getty Images: Jorgen Angel: 23r; Archive Photos: 27; Fin Costello: 2, 4, 6, 10, 13, 16, 19, 21, 23ul, 23ll, 24, 25, 29, 32, 37, 41, 43, 44, 46, 47, 49, 51, 52, 55, 64, 68, 69, 71, 72, 75, 76l, 76r, 80, 87, 88, 89t, 91, 92, 96, 99t, 103, 104, 109, 111, 114, 117, 118, 119t, 121, 126, 128, 131, 136, 141, 143, 144, 147t, 151, 152, 154, 156bl, 159, 160; Ian Dickson: 167ml; Ivan Keeman: 34; Keystone: 122t; Paul Natkin: 42, 50, 79; Ebet Roberts: 84; Pete Still: 54, 67, 101, 156t; Koh Hasebe/Shinko Music: 167mr; David Tan/Shinko Music: 38, 99br, 155; Virginia Turbett: 83.

QPG Collection: 9m, 9r, 9l, 14, 30, 35ur, 35mr, 58, 61, 77t, 89b, 94, 116, 122b, 123, 138ur, 138br, 147bl, 147br, 164bl.

INDEX

Quarto.com

First Published in 2026 by Motorbooks, an imprint of The Quarto Group, 100 Cummings Center, Suite 265-D, Beverly, MA 01915, USA. T (978) 282-9590 F (978) 283-2742

EEA Representation, WTS Tax d.o.o., Žanova ulica 3, 4000 Kranj, Slovenia.
www.wts-tax.si

30 29 28 27 26   1 2 3 4 5

ISBN: 978-0-7603-9923-1

Digital edition published in 2026
eISBN: 978-0-7603-9924-8

Library of Congress Cataloging-in-Publication Data available

Design and page layout: Kelley Galbreath
Cover Image: Fin Costello/Getty Images

Printed in Guangdong, China TT122025

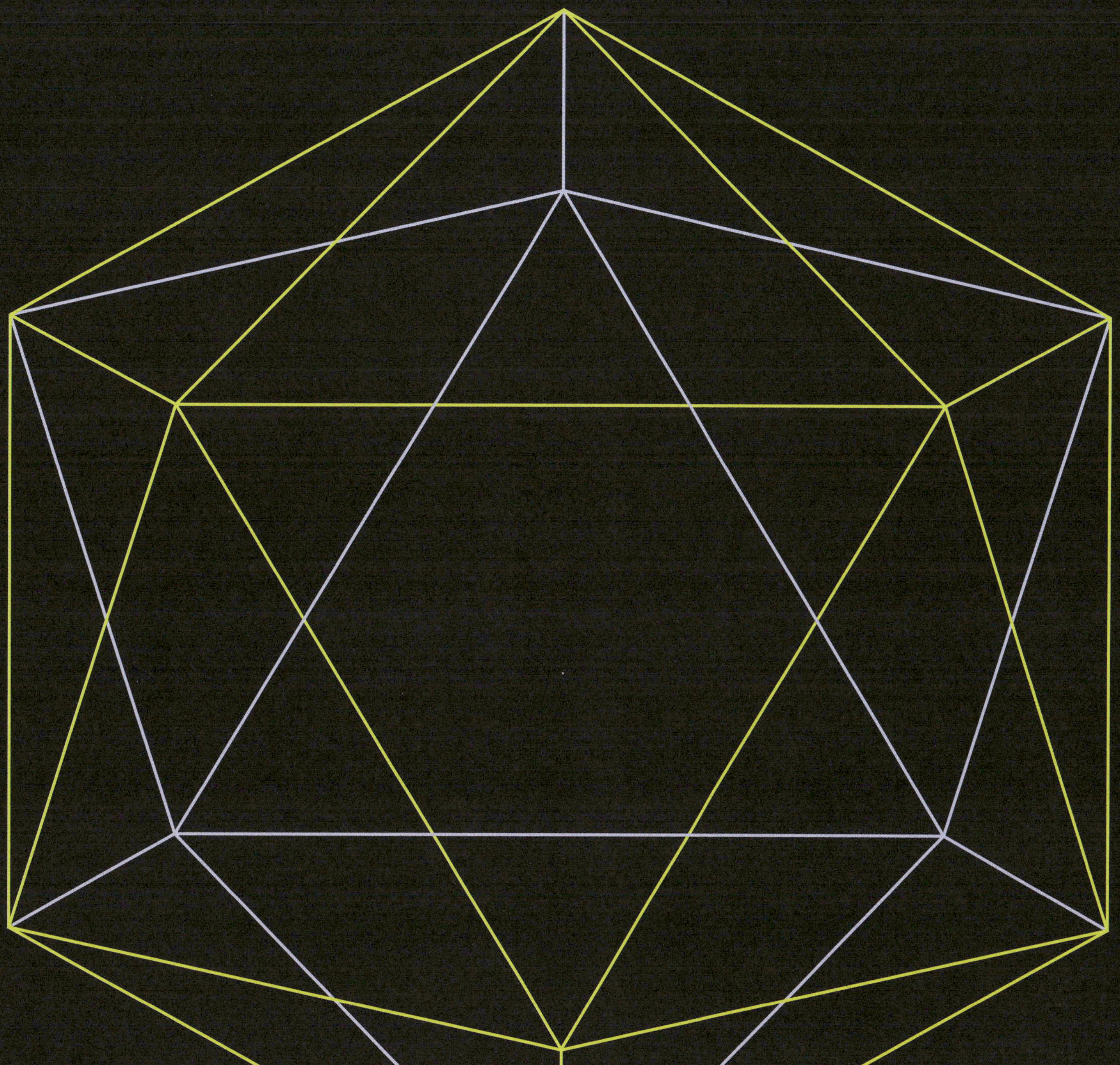